Lifestyles of the Great & Spacious

Lifestyles of the Great & Spacious

Finding Your Path in Lehi's Dream

John Bytheway

SALT LAKE CITY, UTAH

Visit us at DeseretBook.com

Library of Congress Cataloging-in-Publication Data

Bytheway, John, 1962– author.
Lifestyles of the great and spacious / John Bytheway.
pages cm
Includes bibliographical references.
ISBN 978-1-60907-371-8 (paperbound)
1. Lehi's dream—Criticism, interpretation, etc. 2. Tree of life—Symbolic aspects. 3. Symbolism in the Book of Mormon. 4. The Church of Jesus Christ of Latter-day Saints—Doctrines. I. Title.
BX8627.B94 2013
289.3'22—dc23 2012048088

Printed in the United States of America
RR Donnelley, Crawfordsville, IN

10 9 8 7 6 5 4 3 2 1

CONTENTS

ACKNOWLEDGMENTS

Special thanks to Chris Schoebinger, my product director at Deseret Book, for his continuous encouragement and loyalty. I'm also grateful to Leslie Stitt for her editorial skill, to Shauna Gibby for her designing talent, to Rachael Ward for her typesetting work, and to Derk Koldewyn for seeing the production through to the end.

Thanks to my wife, Kim, for reading the early manuscript and making it better, and to all my children for their patience.

I am indebted to Brigham Young University and the BYU Salt Lake Center for allowing me to teach courses on the Book of Mormon over the years and to associate with wonderful students who share with me their own questions, comments, and insights.

Lastly, I'm grateful to my Father in Heaven for His many blessings and many mercies.

INTRODUCTION

Behold, I have dreamed a dream;
or, in other words, I have seen a vision.
—1 Nephi 8:2

It's only thirty-two verses, or 982 words in length (1 Nephi 8:4–35), but it's a life changer—an unforgettable and highly applicable metaphor. We call it Lehi's dream. The basic elements of the dream: the tree of life, the rod of iron, the mists of darkness, and the ominous great and spacious building have become the subject of books, articles, lessons, paintings, plays, and hymns.

With very little effort, we can identify things that happen to us every day that remind us of the dream.

It is, in one instant, specific to Lehi and Sariah's family, and in another, universal to all the sons and daughters of God. Indeed, everything can be found within the dream—light and darkness, love and contention, agency and bondage, purity and filthiness, peer pressure and steadfastness, conformity and individualism, happiness and misery. It's all here. All of life fits into this metaphor.

The Lord chooses his own methods of revelation, and he could have tutored his prophet in many different ways. He could have given Lehi a book to read (which he did in 1 Nephi 1:11), he could have taught him the doctrines and principles within the vision using words alone, or he could have shown him the elements within the dream. But the Lord didn't make Lehi a mere spectator, watching and learning and taking notes from afar. Instead, the Lord taught his prophet by taking him out of the bleachers and placing him right in the middle of the action. Lehi became literally a character within the plot, and he saw himself and his family interacting in this miniature world.

Similarly, we can each find ourselves in this

remarkable dream, which is exactly the purpose of this little book—to help us find ourselves within Lehi's dream. Particular emphasis will be given to the great and spacious building, since it is, in large part, the world in which we currently struggle to survive.

The better we understand Lehi's dream, the better we will be able to hold fast on our way, recognizing the lures, temptations, and mists of darkness for what they are, and arrive—and remain—at the tree of life.

So, here's how we will approach our topic: First, we'll look at Lehi's dream, and each element within it, verse by verse, with ideas on how we might apply what we're learning. Next, we'll try to determine what the voices in the great and spacious building were actually saying, and why they had such power to lure partakers away from the tree. Finally, we'll examine how we might be strong enough to "heed not" the scoffing and derision, and instead seek "tree-of-life moments" in our lives.

1

REASON TO REJOICE AND REASON TO FEAR

And behold, because of the thing which I have seen, I have reason to rejoice in the Lord because of Nephi and also of Sam; for I have reason to suppose that they, and also many of their seed, will be saved. But behold, Laman and Lemuel, I fear exceedingly because of you.
—*1 Nephi 8:3–4*

Thoughts, Insights, and Observations

If the words of John the Beloved are true, "I have no greater joy than to hear that my children walk in truth" (3 John 1:4), then it is also true that no greater sorrow can come than to hear that children walk in darkness. Lehi experienced both, as he witnessed the behavior of his sons Sam, Nephi, Laman, and Lemuel and felt both joy and fear.

The whole reason Lehi felt compelled to share this dream with his sons was because he feared what the vision said about their future. However, he believes his vision is only a prophecy of what *might* be, not necessarily of what *must* be, since, as Lehi concluded, he "did exhort them then with all the feeling of a tender parent" that they would hearken to his words (1 Nephi 8:37).

So while Lehi's dream is a revelation, it was not necessarily a prophecy of his son's future—at least Lehi didn't believe it to be so, or he would not have tried so hard to persuade them to change. A similar example (although fictional) involved the critical question of Ebenezer Scrooge, who asked the Spirit of Christmas Yet to Come, "Are these the shadows of things that Will be, or are they shadows of things that May be only?" (Dickens, *A Christmas Carol,* 143). Scrooge was shown a vision of what might be, unless he changed, which he did. Perhaps Lehi's dream was a warning to Laman and Lemuel of what might be, but with the possibility of a better outcome for them should they choose to change.

Applying the Dream to Our Reality

Some of our sorrows we bring upon ourselves, and some come from watching those we love make poor choices. It is interesting to note that the Book of Mormon story does not begin with a model family that does everything right and keeps all the commandments. Rather it begins with an imperfect family, one might even say a dysfunctional family. In the course of their journey, two sons threaten to kill their brother, and the same sons threaten to kill their own father (that would qualify as dysfunctional).

We can only imagine how thrilled Sariah must be to have an account of her family's problems published among all nations, kindreds, tongues, and peoples. How grateful we are to them, however, for sharing their family trials and triumphs with us. We feel for them, and because of their willingness to share, we find some comfort in knowing that ancient families struggled too.

2

THE WILDERNESS PRECEDES THE PROMISED LAND

For behold, methought I saw in my dream, a dark and dreary wilderness. And it came to pass that I saw a man, and he was dressed in a white robe; and he came and stood before me. And it came to pass that he spake unto me, and bade me follow him. —1 Nephi 8:4–6

Thoughts, Insights, and Observations

As with most things in life, and as attested to in many stories within the scriptures, one must go through the wilderness to get to the promised land. The Fall came before the Atonement, and the Apostasy before the Restoration, and darkness and difficulty often precede light and peace.

While in this wilderness, Lehi saw a man dressed

in a white robe. The phrase "white robe" appears only three times in the Book of Mormon: once here, a second time when Nephi sees an expanded version of the dream and is visited by an angel in a white robe, and once to describe the Savior's attire when he appeared to the righteous children of a different Lehi in the land Bountiful (3 Nephi 11:8). Similarly, the Prophet Joseph Smith saw Moroni, who wore a "loose robe of most exquisite whiteness" (Joseph Smith–History 1:31). Clearly, Lehi trusted this man dressed in a white robe as a messenger from God—a messenger who, unlike Lehi, was not lost, since he asked him to follow, indicating he had a destination or a purpose for Lehi in mind.

> And it came to pass that as I followed him I beheld myself that I was in a dark and dreary waste. And after I had traveled for the space of many hours in darkness, I began to pray unto the Lord that he would have mercy on me, according to the multitude of his tender mercies. (1 Nephi 8:7–8)

This verse has led many students of the scriptures to ask an interesting question: Why would a messenger from God lead someone to a place of darkness?

Actually, the messenger was not leading Lehi *to* a place of darkness, but *through* a place of darkness (a place, we learn later, is symbolic of the Fall). Thus, the appearance of the robed messenger was an act of mercy, not punishment.

Later in the Book of Mormon, Lehi's namesake had another experience with darkness. Lehi and Nephi, the missionary sons of Helaman, were cast into prison. A voice from heaven spoke to their captors, and they were "overshadowed with a cloud of darkness, and an awful solemn fear came upon them" (Helaman 5:28). Eventually, the Lamanites pleaded, "What shall we do, that this cloud of darkness may be removed from overshadowing us?" A fellow prisoner named Aminadab answered, "You must repent, and cry unto the voice, even until ye shall have faith in Christ . . . and when ye shall do this, the cloud of darkness shall be removed from overshadowing you" (Helaman 5:40–41).

Applying the Dream to Our Reality

Faith in Christ dispels darkness, because, as M. Russell Ballard has taught, it's hard to have a negative attitude about *anything* when your life is built on Christ (see *Our Search for Happiness*, 15).

Jeffrey R. Holland referred to Lehi's "white robed" messenger as an angel, who led Lehi "to safety and ultimately to the path of salvation." Elder Holland continued,

> In the course of life all of us spend time in "dark and dreary" places, wildernesses, circumstances of sorrow or fear or discouragement. Our present day is filled with global distress over financial crises, energy problems, terrorist attacks, and natural calamities. These translate into individual and family concerns not only about homes in which to live and food available to eat but also about the ultimate safety and well-being of our children and the latter-day prophecies about our planet. ("The Ministry of Angels," 29)

When dark clouds of trouble hang over us, whether physical or emotional, the answer is the same. Repent and cry unto the voice.

3

AFTER I PRAYED, I BEHELD

And it came to pass after I had prayed unto the Lord I beheld a large and spacious field. —*1 Nephi* 8:9

Thoughts, Insights, and Observations

After Lehi prayed, what was a "dark and dreary waste" became a "large and spacious field." In other words, after his prayer, the lights came on, and Lehi saw his surroundings with clarity for the first time. Prayer brings enlightenment and light.

When we speak of Lehi's dream in our classes and conversations, we often neglect to mention that the dream *began* with a "dark and dreary wilderness." We instead skip ahead to the tree of life, the rod of iron, and so forth. But Lehi's desperation in the dark and dreary wilderness, and his humble prayer for help, are both critical parts of the dream. Dennis Largey has suggested that each element in Lehi's dream is part of a pattern that illustrates our mortal experience and spiritual growth.

> As one follows Christ and learns of him and his plan, one becomes increasingly aware of his or her own mortal and fallen condition. Understanding the need to be saved from this darkness, the necessary cry is for mercy, for every person sins and needs redemption from the Fall. After the cry for mercy the Lord manifests the source of his mercy: a tree which is a representation of the Love of God (see 1 Nephi 11:25). (*The Book of Mormon Reference Companion*, 517)

Because of the Fall, we each find ourselves in a dark and dreary wilderness, and we "are made partakers of misery and woe" (Moses 6:48). In our Latter-day Saint theology, we often refer to the Fall as a fall *forward.* A fall downward, yes, but a fall forward because it moves us along in our spiritual progression. If the Fall is the sickness, then the Atonement of Christ is the cure. What then, is the cure for spiritual darkness? Lehi was about to find out. As he emerged from the darkness, he beheld a marvelous light in the form of a tree.

Applying the Dream to Our Reality

First of all, we remember that Lehi was on a journey. All of us are on a journey. Perhaps it is no accident that the Book of Mormon begins with a journey. The house of Israel had their exodus out of Egypt, and the pioneers had their exodus as well. All of us are going somewhere, and this earth life is only one stop along our eternal path. Lehi's journey began when he met a man in a white robe, who invited him to follow. Lehi followed, and eventually found himself in a dark and dreary waste.

Similarly, we chose to follow our Heavenly Father's plan with Jesus Christ as our Savior, and we chose to follow him. However, we will all have to pass through some dark times in a fallen world. "So, when life gets dark and dreary," the song says, "Don't forget to pray" (*Hymns*, no. 140). Lehi prayed, and the result was illumination to the point that what was first "a dark and dreary wilderness" was now a large and spacious field, "as if it had been a world" (1 Nephi 8:20).

I'll never forget an experience I had one night while driving to a speaking assignment in Vernal, Utah, a town near the Colorado border. I wasn't able to leave my home in Salt Lake until 9 P.M., so I knew I would be traversing the mountains in the dark. What I didn't know was that soon after I left the Salt Lake Valley, I would run into a late April storm. The snow fell so heavily that even with my high-beam headlights ablaze, I could only see a car length or two ahead of me. With my hands wrapped around the steering wheel, I slowed to a crawl, wondering how fast my reaction time would be should a deer suddenly dart across Highway 40. I prayed for safety but I didn't close my eyes, since they were glued to the road. Any previous fears of dozing off during the trip were gone as my adrenal glands were operating at full capacity. After my prayer, my eyes drifted to my GPS. I had almost forgotten it was there! Its tiny screen displayed clearly what lay ahead—things my eyes couldn't see. A gentle left turn, Strawberry

Reservoir on the right, Soldier Creek exit coming up. A calm assurance came over me as I realized I knew exactly where I was. Thousands of eyes in the heavens attached to orbiting satellites were watching me through the dark clouds, and, although it was still dark, it was as if the lights had come on. It was still a long and tense drive, but as I regained a sense of my surroundings, I felt gratitude for all those orbiting eyes looking down on me from above the storm clouds. No matter how dark our circumstances, heavenly eyes are upon us as well. President John Taylor testified, "God lives, and his eyes are over us, and his angels are round and about us, and they are more interested in us than we are in ourselves, ten thousand times, but we do not know it" (in *Journal of Discourses*, 23:221).

4

SWEETNESS AND JOY

And it came to pass that I beheld a tree, whose fruit was desirable to make one happy. And it came to pass that I did go forth and partake of the fruit thereof; and I beheld that it was most sweet, above all that I ever before tasted. Yea, and I beheld that the fruit thereof was white, to exceed all the whiteness that I had ever seen. And as I partook of the fruit thereof it filled my soul with exceedingly great joy; wherefore, I began to be desirous that my family should partake of it also; for I knew that it was desirable above all other fruit. —1 Nephi 8:10–12

Thoughts, Insights, and Observations

You can lead a horse to water, but you cannot make him drink. Similarly, you can lead souls to the tree of life, but you cannot make them eat. We yearn for our friends and often our family members to "go forth and partake" of righteousness, and we are pained when they do not or will not. Lehi beheld the tree, and "did go forth and partake" and it filled his soul with joy.

Lehi used very strong words to describe the fruit of the tree—"most sweet above all that I ever before tasted" and "desirable above all other fruit." Clever marketers also use strong words to advertise their products, but discerning ears can hear that sometimes strong words conceal averageness. For example, if I advertise that my laundry detergent is so effective that "nothing cleans *better* than Super Duper," I'm really saying it's possible that all laundry detergents clean about the same. So, in that case, of course it's true that nothing else cleans *better.* But I'm not really saying much at all about the effectiveness of Super Duper.

Lehi, however, gave us no wiggle room in his description. In unmistakable terms, he described the fruit as the very best he had ever tasted—not "nothing tastes better," but "desirable above all other fruit." As more and more elements of the dream and vision were revealed, the fruit of the tree of life still remained the very best and the most desirable objective in the dream. It was superior. The most wonderful thing available. "Far beyond" anything else (1 Nephi 11:8). Interestingly, Lehi used testimony-bearing language when he expressed that he "knew" it was desirable above all other fruit.

Lehi partook of the fruit that not only satisfied his hunger, but filled his soul with joy. It goes without saying that this was no ordinary fruit, and no ordinary tree. Interestingly, Lehi never referred to the tree as the "tree of life." Not until we come to Nephi's vision of Lehi's dream is the tree described as the "tree of life" and the fruit identified as the "love of God." And yet, somehow Lehi knew before he had even tasted the fruit that the tree was a metaphor of something greater. It was desirable, not just to fill the stomach, but to make one *happy*. Happiness is what all sane people seek, and Lehi had found it.

Lehi had found joy, but his family was suffering. Uprooted from all they had ever known, and now traveling to an unknown destination in an unfamiliar and dangerous wilderness must have shaken them to the core. Doubtless Father Lehi knew of his children's struggles, and just before he died, he took the time to give some final counsel and encouragement to each of his sons.

If you were Lehi, what would you say to your son Jacob? He was born in the wilderness, and he had never seen Jerusalem or the land of his family's inheritance. He experienced the difficulties of the journey, and he must have witnessed the near constant discord within the family. It was in this context that Lehi shared some of his most profound teachings on the Fall. Lehi taught his son, not surprisingly, that there must be "opposition in all things" (2 Nephi 2:11). And perhaps because Jacob had seen such opposition since his earliest years, Lehi also gave him hope with this memorable and oft-quoted verse, "Adam fell that men might be; and men are, that they might have joy" (2 Nephi 2:25). The Prophet Joseph Smith taught:

> Happiness is the object and design of our existence; and will be the end thereof, if we pursue the path that leads to it; and this path is virtue,

uprightness, faithfulness, holiness, and keeping all the commandments of God. (*Teachings*, 255–56)

Applying the Dream to Our Reality

As mortals, we occasionally complain "I'm just not happy," as if that were somehow unique, unusual, or unfair. If we're expecting to be 100 percent happy 100 percent of the time, we're going to be 100 percent disappointed. This life is called a "probationary state" (Alma 12:24). It is not the "state of happiness" that comes after this life (Alma 40:12). Even with a testimony of the gospel, life will have its ups and downs, to be sure. The Savior taught, "in this world your joy is not full, but in me your joy is full" (D&C 101:36). "In him," in Christ, is the only place where the possibility of a fullness of joy lies.

When Lehi discussed the Fall with his son Jacob, he taught, "Men are, that they might have joy." Note the careful wording: "they *might* have joy." I remember one particular day in high school when I was having a rough time. My father said to me, "This too shall pass." And he was right. It did pass. On another day, things were going really well and I was on top of the world. My dad shocked me when he repeated the same words, "This too shall pass." Indeed, on some days, we *might* have joy. Then again, we might not. Those are days of "misery and woe" (Moses 6:48). Each of us experiences what Lehi called opposition in all things. But there is always hope, because joy is possible, and we learn from Lehi's dream that joy is found at the tree of life, and joy is our ultimate destination if we follow the Savior.

5

WHERE SHOULD WE GO?

And as I cast my eyes round about, that perhaps I might discover my family also, I beheld a river of water; and it ran along, and it was near the tree of which I was partaking the fruit. And I looked to behold from whence it came; and I saw the head thereof a little way off; and at the head thereof I beheld your mother Sariah, and Sam, and Nephi; and they stood as if they knew not whither they should go.

—1 Nephi 8:13–14

Thoughts, Insights, and Observations

Lehi had found the lone source of ultimate joy and happiness, and after the humbling and frightening experience of traversing the dark and dreary wilderness, he beheld before him the tree of life. Its fruit was ripe and ready for the taking. And at this point, it wasn't so very hard to come by. All he had to do was go forth and partake. He did partake, and he found maximum sweetness and joy. And it did, in fact, grow on trees.

It's interesting to note the order in which Lehi saw the elements of the dream. The first thing he saw as he emerged from the dark and dreary wilderness, was the tree. After partaking of the fruit, he noticed the river. While looking for the source of the river, he saw a few members of his family, and called to them. At this point, Lehi had not yet seen the rod of iron or the great and spacious building.

When Lehi encountered the tree, he knew that the fruit was "desirable to make one happy" (1 Nephi 8:10). Sariah, Sam, and Nephi, on the other hand, "knew not whither they should go." It appears they weren't moving at all, since Lehi says "they stood."

In the book of Acts, we read about a man of Ethiopia who was reading the book of Esaias (Isaiah) when Philip drew near and said, "Understandest thou what thou readest?" and he responded, "How can I, except some man should guide me?" (Acts 8:30–31; evidently, even those who lived 2,000 years ago sometimes needed help understanding Isaiah). We could all use a guide from time to time, someone who knows. Lehi knew. And he wanted to share what he knew with a loud voice to those he loved most.

Applying the Dream to Our Reality

Each person is born into this world in his or her own unique circumstance. My mother was born into the Church and has ancestors who crossed the plains. My father joined the Church after serving in World War II and witnessing much of the great and spacious building. My mother has remained near the tree her whole life with no desire to go touring. My father saw enough of the great and spacious that when he tasted the fruit of the gospel the contrast was powerful and unmistakable.

Perhaps we could say that each of us has different starting lines in life. Some are born and raised in the great and spacious building and find the tree. Some go through life without knowing anything about the tree, and are kept from the joys of the gospel because they don't know where to look. But once we have tasted of the fruit, or the love of God, as Nephi called it, we can become guides who beckon to others with a loud voice.

Joseph Smith called on all of us to serve as "guides" when he observed from Liberty Jail:

> For there are many yet on the earth among all sects, parties, and denominations, who are blinded by the subtle craftiness of men, whereby they lie in wait to deceive, and who are *only kept from the truth because they know not where to find it*—Therefore, that we should waste and wear out our lives in bringing to light all the hidden things of darkness, wherein we know them; and they are truly manifest from heaven. (D&C 123:12–13; emphasis added)

In this world, it appears that some instinctively know where to go and what will make them happy. Some say, "I've known from my earliest years that God lives. I've never doubted, I've just always known." Others have struggled and suffered and endured and have come later in life to the knowledge of the truth and of what matters most. Still others stand still not knowing where they should go. Our role is simple and was defined by the Savior in seven words: "When thou art converted, strengthen thy brethren" (Luke 22:32).

6

COME UNTO ME

And it came to pass that I beckoned unto them; and I also did say unto them with a loud voice that they should come unto me, and partake of the fruit, which was desirable above all other fruit. And it came to pass that they did come unto me and partake of the fruit also.
—*1 Nephi 8:15–16*

THOUGHTS, INSIGHTS, AND OBSERVATIONS

Notice that Lehi said "come unto me" when he called to his family. We recognize this phrase as one the Savior often used, and the same invitation is repeated by many prophets throughout the scriptures. Interestingly, it is often an invitation to eat. Alma invited, "*Come unto me* and ye shall partake of the fruit of the tree of life; yea, ye shall eat and drink of the bread and the waters of life freely" (Alma 5:34; emphasis added). Jacob the brother of Nephi declared, "*come unto the Holy One of Israel,* and feast upon that which perisheth not, neither can be corrupted, and let your soul delight in fatness" (2 Nephi 9:51; emphasis added). Once again, the Lord invited "*Come unto me* all ye ends of the earth, buy milk and honey, without money and without price" (2 Nephi 26:25; emphasis added).

Along these same lines, have you ever noticed that the Lord never tells anyone to "Go away"? The Lord always invites. To the righteous Nephites and Lamanites he said, "And ye see that I have commanded that none of you should *go away,* but rather have commanded that ye should *come unto me,* that ye might feel and see" (3 Nephi 18:25; emphasis added). No one is on a "go away" list. Nephi observed, "He inviteth them all to *come unto him* and partake of his goodness; and he denieth none that come unto him, black and white, bond and free, male and female; and he remembereth the heathen; and all are alike unto God, both Jew and Gentile" (2 Nephi 26:33; emphasis added).

The opportunity to partake of the tree of life is available to anyone and everyone, if they will only come.

> And it came to pass that I was desirous that Laman and Lemuel should come and partake of the fruit also; wherefore, I cast mine eyes towards the head of the river, that perhaps I might see them. And it came to pass that I saw them, but they would not come unto me and partake of the fruit. (1 Nephi 8:17–18)

Part of Lehi's family was enjoying the fruit, but Lehi wanted all of his family to receive the blessings offered at the tree of life. He saw Laman and Lemuel, and evidently they saw him too—but they *would not* come. This must have been a painful moment for Lehi, a moment to which many modern parents may also relate. This is the moment that caused Lehi to want to share the dream with his family in the first place. Recall that Lehi's retelling of the vision began with this sentence: "But behold, Laman and Lemuel, I fear exceedingly because of you; for behold, methought I saw in my dream, a dark and dreary wilderness . . ." (1 Nephi 8:4).

There is a monumental difference between "*could* not come" and "*would* not come." There was no obstacle in the way, no barrier preventing Laman and Lemuel from making their way toward Lehi and the tree, except their own agency. They *would* not come. Agency is painful. Some choose not to come, some choose not to hear, and some choose not to see.

Jacob may have remembered his older brothers when he taught the people of Nephi: "Wo unto the deaf that *will not hear;* for they shall perish. Wo unto the blind that *will not see;* for they shall perish also (2 Nephi 9:31–32; emphasis added).

After Lehi partook of the fruit, which Nephi later tells us represents the love of God (1 Nephi 11:22), Lehi's thoughts went to his family—but they didn't stop there. The Prophet Joseph Smith taught: "A man filled with the love of God is not content with blessing his family alone, but ranges through the whole world, anxious to bless the whole human race" (*History of the Church*, 4:227).

A textbook example of effect of the love of God on one's heart can be found in the story of Lehi's grandson, Enos. Enos went out to hunt, and, as he reflected on his father Jacob's teachings, he pondered the state of his own soul. He eventually lost all interest in hunting, and instead spent the day in fervent prayer. First he prayed for himself, and once the Lord assured him concerning the welfare of his soul, he "began to feel a desire for the welfare of [his] brethren, the Nephites" (Enos 1:9). Following the Lord's answer concerning the Nephites, he prayed with "many long strugglings" for the Lamanites (Enos 1:11). Once the Lord assured him concerning the Lamanites, he prayed for the safety of the many records they had been keeping, and that they might be preserved for the benefit of Lamanites in the future. Enos could have stopped praying once he received an answer concerning his own soul, but the "love of God" in his heart wouldn't let him. It "rang[ed] through the whole world" (*History of the Church*, 4:227).

Applying the Dream to Our Reality

What happens when we come across something absolutely wonderful? Our first impulse is to share. How many times have you heard yourself say, "Oh, you have got to try this," or, "You have to hear this song," or, "I have a book you've got to read!" We love to share our joy with others, and Lehi was no different. Lehi's immediate reaction after tasting the fruit was, "Where is my family?" Sariah, Sam, and Nephi accepted Lehi's invitation, but Laman and Lemuel did not. But would any of us believe that Lehi regretted offering to others what he had found? Not for a moment. Similarly, our regrets will likely be that we didn't share enough, not that we shared too often.

After blessing our family, the love of God moves us into even broader circles. There are many different motives for doing missionary work, but perhaps Alma the Younger's is the best and highest. Although he's expressing his views hundreds of years after Lehi's dream, he uses the tree-of-life metaphor to express his desire to share the gospel—not to feel what he has felt, but to *taste* what he had *tasted:* "Yea, and from that time even until now, I have labored without ceasing, that I might bring souls unto repentance; that I might bring them to taste of the exceeding joy of which I did taste; that they might also be born of God, and be filled with the Holy Ghost" (Alma 36:24).

7

THE ROD OF IRON AND THE PATH

And I beheld a rod of iron, and it extended along the bank of the river, and led to the tree by which I stood. And I also beheld a strait and narrow path, which came along by the rod of iron, even to the tree by which I stood; and it also led by the head of the fountain, unto a large and spacious field, as if it had been a world. And I saw numberless concourses of people, many of whom were pressing forward, that they might obtain the path which led unto the tree by which I stood. —1 Nephi 8:19–21

Thoughts, Insights, and Observations

In this verse we are introduced to two new elements within the vision. A rod of iron and a strait and narrow path. We may assume the strait and narrow path ran parallel to the rod of iron since it "came along" and "led to" the tree.

The "strait and narrow" is a biblical metaphor shared by all Christians and is often mentioned in our religious discussions and lessons. But Lehi's dream adds a new element to the strait and narrow path. Lehi saw a rod of iron that was absolutely essential for staying on the path should any hazards (yet unnamed) arise.

The rod of iron had more than one function. Not only did the rod assist in directing one toward the tree, but it also protected those who held onto it from falling into the river—a river, we discover later, that is symbolic of the "depths of hell." Because it led to the tree, we might call the rod of iron a "guide-rail." Because it also protected travelers from falling into the river, we might also call it a "guardrail."

So concerning this path, let's get this strait—or is it straight? The strait and narrow path is both *strait* and *straight.* It is strait, because it is narrow and restricted, like a strait jacket that limits one's movement. Those who traverse the gospel path find it *strait,* because some things must be left behind. It is also *straight,* meaning in direction, because God does not deviate—he "cannot walk in crooked paths; neither doth he vary from that which he hath said; neither hath he a shadow of turning from the right to the left, or from that which is right to that which is wrong" (Alma 7:20).

Lehi beheld that the path led to a large and spacious field—so large, in fact, that Lehi likened it to the world. Lehi also saw "numberless concourses of people," who were looking for the path that led to the tree. Interestingly, this is the first time Lehi mentions other people outside his own family. This is the moment when Lehi's dream becomes about more than just Lehi's family—it's about you and me, it's about all of us.

You may have noticed another interesting insight in these two verses. While Lehi was describing these additional parts of the dream, note that his observation post didn't change. He didn't move an inch. Lehi said three separate times, "the tree *by which I stood.*" Not just "the tree," but the tree *by which I stood.* Once Lehi arrived in this sacred place, he wasn't about to leave. He was there to stay, and perhaps he wanted his listeners to know it. Similarly, Peter's response to the Savior's question, "Will ye also go away?" was, "To whom shall we go?" (John 6:67–68). Lehi had tasted the love of God, delicious above anything he had ever before tasted—where else would he go?

Applying the Dream to Our Reality

We emphasize and will continue to emphasize the importance of "staying on the straight and narrow," but Lehi's additional element gives us something to hold on to that is "strong, and bright, and true" (*Hymns*, no. 274). If we ever get comfortable thinking, "I'm okay because I'm on the path," we might ask ourselves about our grip. In the dream, the iron rod kept people from falling. Symbolically, it protects us from falling away.

We travel dozens of paths every week, while at school, while shopping or running errands, or while out on the town. We go up and down stairs, over bridges, and across ramps. Many of these walkways are accompanied by metal railings. But most of us rarely hold onto the railings, in fact, we are probably so preoccupied with getting where we're going that we aren't even aware they are there. So it's easy to take railings for granted, to regard them as invisible almost, unless we really need them.

President Ezra Taft Benson said:

> However diligent we may be in other areas, certain blessings are to be found only in the scriptures, only in coming to the word of the Lord and holding fast to it as we make our way through the mists of darkness to the tree of life. ("The Power of the Word," 82)

We need the iron rod. Nephi taught his brothers that the iron rod symbolized "the word of God" (1 Nephi 15:24). The rod of iron didn't do anyone any good unless they held onto it. Similarly, the word of God does us no good unless we hold onto it, or hear and hearken. Lehi's dream compels us to ask, "Is this journey of mortality just a pleasant stroll, completely devoid of any danger? And are we content to leave our scriptures comfortably on the nightstand, or are we holding on for dear life?" When moving along the gospel path, it's important to hold on right now, whether it feels critical or not, rather than wait until some crisis arises to finally get a grip.

It's possible to be a member of the Church, going to meetings, participating in class, being "on the path," and feeling quite safe and secure, but not really holding fast to the word of God, or not regularly studying the scriptures and the words of the living prophets. As Lehi's description continues, another hazard is introduced that makes the rod of iron not just convenient, but indispensable in the journey toward the tree of life.

8

THE MIST OF DARKNESS

And it came to pass that they did come forth, and commence in the path which led to the tree. And it came to pass that there arose a mist of darkness; yea, even an exceedingly great mist of darkness, insomuch that they who had commenced in the path did lose their way, that they wandered off and were lost. —1 Nephi 8:22–23

Thoughts, Insights, and Observations

When the numberless concourses of people commenced in the path, they were met with blinding opposition. Not a blinding *light,* in this case, but a blinding *darkness.* And it wasn't merely a mist of darkness, as we often abbreviate the phrase, but an "exceedingly great" mist of darkness, which caused them to lose their way. Hugh Nibley helps us imagine how frightening a "great mist of darkness" would be to a desert traveler:

> Of all the images that haunt the early Arab poets this is by all odds the commonest; it is the standard nightmare of the Arab; and it is the supreme boast of every poet that he has traveled long distances through dark and dreary wastes all alone. Invariably darkness is given as the main source of terror (the heat and glare of the day, though nearly always mentioned, are given second place), and the culminating horror is almost always a "mist of darkness," a depressing mixture of dust, and clammy fog, which, added to the night, completes the confusion of any who wander in the waste. Quite contrary to what one would expect, these dank mists are described by travelers in all parts of Arabia, and al-Ajajj, one of the greatest of early desert poets, tells how a "mist of darkness" makes it impossible for him to continue a journey to Damascus. In its nature and effect Lehi's "mist of darkness" (1 Nephi

> 8:23) conforms to this strange phenomenon most exactly. (*Lehi in the Desert,* 47–48)

Scripturally speaking, "light" is synonymous with knowledge, as in "The glory of God is intelligence, or, in other words, light and truth" (D&C 93:36). Darkness means lack of knowledge or ignorance as in "he that hateth his brother is in darkness, and walketh in darkness, and knoweth not whither he goeth, because that darkness hath blinded his eyes" (1 John 2:11). Clearly, this mist wasn't just a mist *in* the darkness, since the setting of this dream is in broad daylight, but a mist *of* darkness. Lehi was not describing a light-colored mist, like steam or fog, but a mist of dark smoke that blinds, and losing one's ability to see while in the middle of a treacherous journey changes everything.

Another consequence we might consider as we ponder the impact of the mist of darkness is loneliness. A thick mist of darkness would isolate travelers from all the others on the path. Before the mist arose, there was at least the comfort of "strength in numbers" since we are told that many of the "numberless concourses" pressed forward to obtain the path that led to the tree.

The mist of darkness would, in effect, make them alone in the dark—a place where souls are more vulnerable to temptation. So what was already "dark and dreary" became "*lone* and dreary" as well.

Also, although we benefit greatly from the positive influence of our brothers and sisters who surround us on the straight and narrow, eventually each of us discover that we cannot endure on borrowed light, or rely solely on positive peer pressure from others to see us through. Pressing forward on the path will, at some point, become an individual effort and an individual decision.

Lehi first mentioned the rod of iron in verse 20, the same verse in which he mentioned the strait and narrow path, but it appears that travelers paid little attention to the iron rod until its presence became critical. You'll notice that Lehi saw numberless concourses of people who were eager to "obtain the path" (verse 21). But it was only after the mist of darkness arose that, suddenly, their objective changed. The next group Lehi mentioned came forward—not with the objective to "obtain the path," but to catch "hold of the end of the rod of iron" (verse 24).

The mist of darkness helps illustrate a point made earlier, but with the arrival of the darkness is even more crucial: *It is possible to be on the path, but not holding the rod.* The rod of iron becomes essential when the darkness comes. It is the only way to continue to the tree. Before, it was an unused benefit. Now, it is the only way to make progress. The dream testifies that those who were merely on the path but not holding to the rod were lost.

> And it came to pass that I beheld others pressing forward, and they came forth and caught hold of the end of the rod of iron; and they did press forward through the mist of darkness, clinging to the rod of iron, even until they did come forth and partake of the fruit of the tree. (1 Nephi 8:24)

This group, the "others pressing forward," did not merely get their feet on the path, but "caught hold of the rod of iron," enabling them to press forward even while blinded by the exceedingly great mist of darkness. With their guide-rail and guardrail in hand, they eventually arrived at the tree of life.

Applying the Dream to Our Reality

Nephi described the mist of darkness in terms of what it represents and of its effect on mankind in chilling terms:

> And the mists of darkness are the temptations of the devil, which blindeth the eyes, and hardeneth the hearts of the children of men, and leadeth them away into broad roads, that they perish and are lost. (1 Nephi 12:17)

The rod of iron is the antidote to the mists of darkness—it enables the blind or those who are surrounded by darkness to "see" where they're going. If you've ever visited a large cave, like Timpanogos Cave, or the Sitting Bull Crystal Caverns near Mount Rushmore, you may have experienced the frightening thrill of being instantly immersed in total blackness when the tour guide douses the lights. You may have noticed that your immediate reaction is to reach for something to hold onto (which is why I always take my wife). Most often the caves are equipped with railings, or "rods of iron," to lead you along the invisible path out of darkness and into safety and light. Should the power suddenly go out during your cave visit, you could feel your way out because of the railings.

Iron is a symbol of hardness, durability, strength, and firmness. I've participated in many Lehi's dream reenactments at youth conferences where a heavy rope was used to symbolize the iron rod. The problem is, a rope can be cut, bent, or moved, and one person can actually move another off the path by yanking the rope. (It's fairly easy to imagine that happening at a youth conference, isn't it?) If you were on the edge of a cliff, or by a river of filthy water, a rope would not make you feel nearly as safe as a rod of iron. A rod of iron is steadfast and immovable!

The benefits of holding fast to the rod of iron were articulated by Nephi to his brothers. Nephi mentioned not only the iron rod's darkness-piercing properties, but its dart-quenching ability:

> I said unto them that it was the word of God; and whoso would hearken unto the word of God, and would hold fast unto it, they would never perish; neither could the temptations and the fiery darts of the adversary overpower them

> unto blindness, to lead them away to destruction. (1 Nephi 15:24)

The Lord wants every part of us, doesn't he? He wants *both feet* on the strait and narrow, he wants *both hands* on the rod of iron, and he wants us to serve with our heart, might, mind, and strength. Elder Neal A. Maxwell combined Paul's "armor of God" imagery (see Ephesians 6:11–17) with the metaphor of the "tree of life" when he observed:

> Real disciples absorb the fiery darts of the adversary by holding aloft the quenching shield of faith with one hand, while holding to the iron rod with the other. There should be no mistaking; it will take both hands! ("Overcome . . . Even as I Also Overcame," 70)

It's probably safe to assume that anyone who is currently sitting down reading a Church book is "on the path," especially when there are so many other things they could be doing. But Lehi was teaching us to beware of the complacency that may come with being merely "on the path." Remember, Lehi observed, "They who had commenced in the path did lose their way"

(1 Nephi 8:23). In our own minds, we can ponder what it means to be not only on the path, but clinging to, and continually holding fast to the iron rod.

You might have noticed that Lehi's dream uses several "C" words to describe interaction and involvement with the path and the rod of iron:

Commence (1 Nephi 8:22)
Cling (1 Nephi 8:24)
Continue (1 Nephi 8:30)

Those who *commenced* in the path, but never grasped the iron rod were eventually lost. Another group got on the path, caught hold of the iron rod and were *clinging* to it through the mists of darkness, but apparently let go after they arrived at the tree of life because they were ashamed. Others *continually held fast,* and, it appears, remained at the tree. David A. Bednar commented on the importance of the word "continually":

> Clinging to the rod of iron suggests to me only occasional "bursts" of study or irregular dipping rather than consistent, ongoing immersion in the word of God. In verse 30 we read about a third group of people who pressed forward continually

> holding fast to the rod of iron until they came forth and fell down and partook of the fruit of the tree. The key phrase in this verse is "continually holding fast" to the rod of iron . . . Perhaps this third group of people consistently read and studied and searched the words of Christ . . . This is the group you and I should strive to join. (*Increase in Learning,* 142)

Another way of saying "continually holding fast" is "never letting go." If you are continually holding fast, you are unable to touch that which is evil or unclean. Moroni, in the fifth to last verse in the entire Book of Mormon counseled, "And again I would exhort you that ye would come unto Christ, and lay hold upon every good gift, and touch not the evil gift, nor the unclean thing" (Moroni 10:30).

9

THE GREAT AND SPACIOUS BUILDING

And after they had partaken of the fruit of the tree they did cast their eyes about as if they were ashamed. And I also cast my eyes round about, and beheld, on the other side of the river of water, a great and spacious building; and it stood as it were in the air, high above the earth. —*1 Nephi 8:25–26*

THOUGHTS, INSIGHTS, AND OBSERVATIONS

This verse describes a pivotal, critical moment—perhaps more important than any other moment in the dream, at least for this group of one-time partakers. Notice that it was *after* they ate of the fruit that they looked around. What were they looking for? Were they looking for approval? Were they wondering, "Does anyone know what I'm doing?" Or perhaps they could hear something coming from the other side of the river, and were looking for the source. In any event, it was only *after looking around* that they became ashamed. The thought, "What do others think of what I'm doing?" is a powerful influencer. Once Lehi saw that those partaking were ashamed, he also looked around to find the cause of their embarrassment, and this was when he first laid eyes on the great and spacious building.

The great and spacious building, remarkably, was "in the air." Nephi points out that the great and spacious building was the "pride of the world" (1 Nephi 11:36). Pride is haughty, lifted up, high and mighty, above the crowd, looking down on everyone and everything.

We can draw a few interesting conclusions from the description of the great and spacious building, particularly the fact that it stood, as it were, "in the air." Attached to the phrase "in the air," is footnote 26c, which takes us to Ephesians 2:2, and Paul's rather strange name for Satan, "the prince of the power of the air." Elder Bruce R. McConkie explained this nickname as "an idiomatic expression indicating Satan's rule and dominance in 'this world,' in, as it were, the very air around us" (*Doctrinal New Testament Commentary*, vol. 2, 499).

If we visualize the great and spacious building in a twenty-first century context, we might imagine a rooftop cluttered with antennas, satellite dishes, cell phone towers, and wi-fi routers. Technology can be used as both a tool and a weapon. Sadly, today, Satan's influence is literally "in the air" with some of the worst images, sounds, and movies the world has to offer saturating the airwaves. Even in the most remote location on earth, where nature is pure and pristine, it seems Satan's influence is still "in the air." Elder Quentin L. Cook related:

> President Dieter F. Uchtdorf and I were recently in an Amazon jungle village and observed satellite dishes even on some of the small, simply built huts. We rejoiced at the wonderful information available in this remote area. We also recognized there is virtually no place on earth that cannot be impacted by salacious, immoral, and

> titillating images. This is one reason why pornography has become such a plague in our day. ("Can Ye Feel So Now?" 8)

Another interesting observation involves the great and spacious building's altitude, seemingly rising above the mists of darkness that were blanketing the ground. If the mists of darkness really are the temptations of the devil, we can surmise a bit of his strategy. S. Michael Wilcox observed:

> There are three things in Lehi's dream that are obscured by the mist and that correspond to the reality of our mortal lives. Satan does not want us to see the tree of life, which we are told symbolizes the love of God. He does not want us to perceive the rod of iron, or the word of God, which will keep us on the path when the tree is lost from our view. He is also desirous that we know nothing of the filthy river or the consequences of misery, both temporal and eternal, which come for those who leave the path. . . . The only major symbol in Lehi's dream that Lucifer does not want to hide is the spacious building,

> which symbolizes pride and the vain things of the world. (*Don't Leap with the Sheep*, 8–9)

Another conclusion often drawn from the description of this floating building is that it has no foundation. Any building with no foundation will eventually fall. A building with no foundation is temporary, to say the least. It's not going to be there forever.

Applying the Dream to Our Reality

We can be blessed by pondering what is real and lasting in our lives and what is merely temporary. Elder John H. Groberg observed that the things that are eternal are *real,* and the things that are temporary are *not real* in the sense that they are not lasting. Temporary things, like the great and spacious building, will eventually decay, die, crumble, or disappear:

> When I first began serving as temple president, I often heard people say, "I wish I didn't have to leave the temple, with its peace and quiet, and go back into the real world, with its noise and frustration." I tended to agree with them but for some reason felt uneasy with that thought and

prayed to know why. One day something special happened. I can't say exactly where or how the words or feelings came, but the concept was clear: "That which lasts forever is real; that which does not last forever is not real. The temple is the real world, not this temporal one." From then on, whenever I heard someone say they were sorry to have to leave the temple and go back into the real world, I would take them aside and say something like the following: I understand your feelings, but actually, it is the other way around. You are not leaving the temple and going back into the real world, you are leaving the real world (the temple) and going back into the unreal (temporary) world. Only that which lasts forever is real. That which is done in the temple lasts forever; therefore, the temple is the real world. Most of what we experience "out there," such as sickness, wealth, poverty, fame, etc., lasts for only a short period of time, so it is not the real world. Because you have been in the temple, however, you can take the truths of the real world with you as you live in the temporary world. As you do, you will see more clearly that which is important (real,

> or eternal) and that which is less important (unreal, temporal, or temporary). This view of things will increase your peace, understanding, and joy. (*Refuge and Reality*, 3–4)

At this point in Lehi's narrative, we don't know exactly why those who partook of the tree of life were ashamed, only that it had something to do with what they saw when they turned around—the building they beheld behind them *after* they partook.

It's interesting that Satan often makes his appearance after great spiritual experiences. He wants us to discount, dismiss, and explain away any event that has drawn us closer to God and that has allowed us to taste the exquisite fruit that represents the love of God. For example, immediately after the spectacular and undeniable signs of the birth of Christ prophesied by Samuel the Lamanite (among which was "a day and a night and a day" with no darkness—a pretty hard sign to fake), Satan showed up to put his spin on the whole thing: "And it came to pass that from this time forth there began to be lyings sent forth among the people, by Satan, to harden their hearts, to the intent that they might not believe in those signs and wonders which they had seen" (3 Nephi 1:22).

Joseph Fielding McConkie and Robert L. Millet explain the same phenomenon:

> Satan always seeks to sow lies whenever there has been a great manifestation of the truth. He tries desperately to confuse, to confound, to complicate things. He works diligently to harden hearts against the plain verities of heaven as well as against the signs and wonders which are evident among believers. (*Doctrinal Commentary on the Book of Mormon*, 4:9)

It would be helpful for each of us to be aware of this particular strategy of Satan. When we experience a wonderful spiritual feast, when we taste the fruit of the tree of life and are filled with joy, we might be wary that Satan will try to get us to rethink or dismiss it.

Perhaps this is one reason why Latter-day Saints are counseled to record their spiritual experiences, not only for their benefit, but for the benefit of their children. We are counseled to record our witness of the hand of the Lord in our lives because the day may come when we may begin to forget what we have experienced. Or we may wonder if what we once accepted as spiritual experiences were only our imagination. This could be the first step on a "strange road" or a "forbidden path," a course which may allow the mists of darkness to blind us to what the Lord has done for us throughout our lives.

A key, critical moment—*perhaps the most critical and pivotal moment in all of Lehi's dream*—is in between the words *tree* and *they* in verse 25. It is the instant when those who had tasted the fruit turned and faced the scoffers. Every member of the Church will face this moment. What will they do? How much will popular opinion affect them?

As a parent, I must prepare my own children for that moment when all they hold dear is called into question by a mob across the way. Will they stand firm? Will they have enough of a testimony to say within themselves, *I don't care what those guys think, this is delicious!* and continue to partake? Every family prayer, every home evening, every gospel discussion where the Spirit is present might add just a little more strength to their spiritual backbone, which could be critical in preparing them for that inevitable confrontation with the great and spacious building.

When we think of those who dropped their heads in shame because of the mocking, we are left to wonder what might have happened had they acted differently in that singular moment with eternal consequences. How different the outcome would have been had they simply turned their back on the building, faced the tree, and continued to partake!

Evidently peer pressure and the pride of the world are powerful enough to persuade some to leave the tree, even after tasting the fruit and feeling the joy. Perhaps we also learn that we must be careful guardians of our spiritual experiences, and not look to the world for their evaluation or their approval.

10

ATTITUDE OF MOCKING

And it was filled with people, both old and young, both male and female; and their manner of dress was exceedingly fine; and they were in the attitude of mocking and pointing their fingers towards those who had come at and were partaking of the fruit. And after they had tasted of the fruit they were ashamed, because of those that were scoffing at them; and they fell away into forbidden paths and were lost. —1 Nephi 8:27–28

Thoughts, Insights, and Observations

The first thing Lehi noticed about the tenants of the great and spacious building was their manner of dress. "Costly apparel" is a common phrase used in the

Book of Mormon to describe wealth, but more specifically, materialism. Since cars, speed boats, electronics, recreational vehicles, and so forth had yet to be invented, wealth and the love of money are usually described in terms of apparel, such as costly clothes and jewelry.

Isaiah spent nearly an entire chapter condemning the daughters of Zion for their jewelry and adornments, which he described in great detail (see 2 Nephi 13:16–26). Isaiah used the phrase "the daughters of Zion" as a symbol for all of us (male and female), along with the symbol of the bridegroom to represent Christ. The reason Isaiah condemned the daughters of Zion was because their adornments and their flirtatious behavior was evidence that they were trying to attract other lovers when they were betrothed to Christ (can you imagine anything more hurtful?). In other words, we are unfaithful to Christ when our riches become our love and the object of our worship.

In addition, costly apparel is condemned because we might be tempted to accumulate wealth at the expense of our neighbor. Moroni asks, "Why do ye adorn yourselves with that which hath no life, and yet suffer the hungry, and the needy, and the naked, and the sick and the afflicted [who have life] to pass by you, and notice them not?" (Mormon 8:39). To put it another way, "you're treating things like people, and people like things." The Savior pled with us to love one another, not to love our possessions more than others.

Lehi also described what the occupants of the building were doing: They were "mocking," "pointing their fingers," and "scoffing." This ridicule caused those who had partaken of the fruit to be ashamed. It's hard to believe that anyone could be ashamed of something so wonderful, so exquisite, and so fulfilling beyond anything else available as the fruit of the tree of life, but that is the danger if we become preoccupied with popular opinion and the "praise of the world."

Let's consider for a moment the impact of the noise coming from the great and spacious building for those who were still on the path. We often speak of the main effect of the mist of darkness as "blinding the eyes" of those making their way. But there is nothing described in Lehi's dream that would affect the sojourner's *hearing.* We can surmise that the nearer the people came to the tree of life, the more they could hear the scoffing from the great and spacious building.

We can only imagine the feelings we might have were we in their place—being overcome by the mists of darkness, being unable to see where we were going, feeling alone and cut off from others, having to grope our way through the mists, all the while being assailed by the mocking, scoffing, and derision from the great and spacious building. Clearly, the journey to the tree of life was not (and is not) a walk in the park.

Applying the Dream to Our Reality

Like those who were drawing nearer and nearer to the tree, we may expect the opposition to get louder and louder. Perhaps Satan works harder on us the closer we get to where we ought to be.

One woman told of a particularly difficult situation at her place of employment, and how the Spirit whispered to her five words from Lehi's dream that made a dramatic difference. This quiet piece of inspiration about a scriptural story had an immediate application that gave her perspective, peace, and power:

> I had worked in an office for several years, and had firmly established my reputation as a "G-Rated" person. No one told questionable jokes around me, and when they did swear, they always apologized to me. The ladies in the office dressed very well, and, although my clothes were neat and clean, I felt plain in comparison. I was able to interact amicably with my coworkers, but I was conspicuously left out of their after-work socializing. This would bother me from time to time, as I felt excluded, but I reminded myself that their after-work activities usually involved bars.
>
> One day I was told that some of the ladies in the office had considered doing something with me, to which one of them commented, "There are only so many churches in Baltimore." I could feel the derision and contempt in her comment.
>
> What really surprised me was how I was hurt by her remark. I told myself I should be glad that she knew that I wouldn't go to bars. So why did it hurt? I struggled with the stinging remark, and

> considered going out with them so I could fit in. I told myself I could go to the bars, and just not drink. I would belong. Still, that option didn't feel right.
>
> As I wrestled with my hurt feelings, and the resulting confusion, a quiet voice in my mind whispered, "the great and spacious building" (1 Nephi 8:26). I was filled with the image of Lehi's dream and the people in the "great and spacious building."
>
> I saw my experience with new clarity as I likened this scripture unto myself. I saw myself being tempted to let go of the iron rod. I felt for a brief moment I was in danger of falling into forbidden paths and becoming lost. I felt a renewed determination that I would not heed the scorners.
>
> I also found a renewed testimony of the importance of studying the scriptures. Only by reading and studying these sacred words can we draw upon them for strength in time of need. ("Living by the Scriptures," *Church News*)

Two "tastes," we might say, competing for the same soul. For some, being mocked is so "distasteful," that they forget the exquisite taste of the fruit of the tree of life. Keeping the memory of the tree of life is a great protection.

There is an old saying that "wise men learn from experience, but super wise men learn from others' experience" (George I. Cannon, "Live to Make Good Memories"). The scriptures are preserved to "enlarge the memory" of the people who read them (Alma 37:8). When the scriptures are treasured up in our minds, we benefit not only from wisdom gained in our past, but from the wisdom and experience of others as well.

11

FELL DOWN AND PARTOOK

And now I, Nephi, do not speak all the words of my father. But, to be short in writing, behold, he saw other multitudes pressing forward; and they came and caught hold of the end of the rod of iron; and they did press their way forward, continually holding fast to the rod of iron, until they came forth and fell down and partook of the fruit of the tree. —1 Nephi 8:29–30

Thoughts, Insights, and Observations

Happily, Lehi also saw "multitudes," yes, *multitudes* who pressed forward to the tree, partook, and, we presume, stayed. We learn from this detail that the Lord is not like an impatient college professor eager to weed out the stragglers in his class so that he can flunk them and advance only a chosen few. Multitudes will be saved.

Lehi adds an interesting phrase in describing this group. They "fell down" once they arrived at the tree. Were they kneeling in worship? Perhaps. Were they exhausted because of the difficulty of staying the course? Maybe. Maybe both. We know that the tree of life is a representation of the love of God, and we know that "God so loved the world, that he gave his only begotten Son" (John 3:16).

A caution: When interpreting parables, allegories, and analogies such as Lehi's dream, we should avoid the temptation to be overly specific in defining what means what. While it is true that the fruit is the love of God, and the iron rod is the word of God, it is also true that the tree is Christ, the fruit is Christ, and the iron rod is Christ. How do we know this? From the angel speaking to Nephi.

In trying to define the tree, remember the interesting conversation Nephi had with the Spirit (1 Nephi 11:4–6).

Spirit: "Believest thou that thy Father saw the tree?"

Nephi: "Yea . . ."

Spirit (rejoicing with a loud voice): "Blessed art thou, Nephi, because thou believest in the Son of the most high God."

This is a pretty clear indication that the tree was, among other things, a symbol of Christ. After the angel showed Nephi events surrounding the birth of Christ, the angel immediately asked, "Knowest thou the meaning of the tree which thy father saw?" (1 Nephi 11:21). It is as if the angel were saying, "*Now* do you know the meaning of the tree?"

Jeffrey R. Holland taught, "The Spirit made explicit that the Tree of Life and its precious fruit are symbols of Christ's redemption" (*Christ and the New Covenant*, 160). So when the people "fell down" at the tree, they fell down to worship. Wayne Brickey has written:

> When telling his family about his dream, Lehi was careful to mention this detail about falling before the tree. Before our Friend and his ample tree, we instinctively kneel. How can we stand before such fortune? Though we realize

> that countless others have rallied to him by covenant, we marvel to know that this is a personal matter. The fruit is personally *from* him, and it is personally *for* us. Worshiping, we taste a life-giving sweetness exceeding anything the world can grow or know. We bask in this greatest of all friendships (1 Nephi 11:21–22; Romans 5:5). Arising, we turn to our loved ones and do what Lehi did. We share with them an inviting home.

He then added, "[Lehi] invited Christ into his family. And then he invited his family to Christ" (*Inviting Him In*, 220).

Applying the Dream to Our Reality

More than once as a bishop, I've had someone tell me, "I'm just afraid I'm not going to make it," or "I'm not good enough," or "I can't do it." In those cases I like to respond, "You're right. You're absolutely right. You can't make it, and neither can I. Not by ourselves, anyway." Somehow, when sincere Latter-day Saints formulate a self-condemning sentence like that, they have momentarily forgotten that Christ is the Savior, and he is mighty to save. He also knows we can't do it on our own, and that although we sometimes drift and murmur and rebel, he just keeps inviting us back to him. In fact, he invites us back to the sacrament table to renew the covenant and the effect of baptism every single week. What mercy!

As we all know, the Lord said, "For behold, this is my work and my glory—to bring to pass the immortality and eternal life of man" (Moses 1:39). He has assured us of this many times, "I am able to do mine own work" (2 Nephi 27:21).

Lehi's dream gives us optimistic insight about the Lord's level of success in his saving work when he describes the "multitudes" who partake and remain at the tree of life. Not "a handful of souls" or "only a few" or "hardly anyone," but "multitudes." Robert L. Millet referred to Lehi's dream as the "Parable of the Paths" when he taught:

> The third group of people in the Parable of the Paths press forward and take hold of the iron rod. How many did so? *Multitudes!* . . . Who can count the number of saved beings in eternity? Our God, who is triumphant in all battles against the forces of evil, will surely be victorious in the

numbers of his children who will be saved. (*Lehi's Dream*, 54)

When President Joseph F. Smith recorded his vision of the redemption of the dead, he described more than multitudes, but an "*innumerable* company of the spirits of the just, who had been faithful in the testimony of Jesus while they lived in mortality" (D&C 138:12; emphasis added).

So, it's true. I can't make it, and you can't make it. Not on our own. But Jesus Christ can make it, and make us, or *re*make us into beings that can be worthy to partake and remain with him at the tree of life.

12

STRAIGHT TO THE GREAT AND SPACIOUS

And he also saw other multitudes feeling their way towards that great and spacious building. And it came to pass that many were drowned in the depths of the fountain; and many were lost from his view, wandering in strange roads. And great was the multitude that did enter into that strange building. And after they did enter into that building they did point the finger of corn at me and those that were partaking of the fruit also; but we heeded them not. These are the words of my father: For as many as heeded them, had fallen away. And Laman and Lemuel partook not of the fruit, said my father.

—1 Nephi 8:31–35

Thoughts, Insights, and Observations

The fourth group Lehi saw seemingly had no interest in the tree of life, but went straight toward the great and spacious—"feeling their way" along. Some were drowned, and some wandered in strange roads, and some arrived at the building and joined the chorus of taunters.

It seems a little odd, doesn't it? After they entered the building, they pointed the finger of scorn. Didn't they want to look around? After all, it was a spacious building! With all that space, it must have had many rooms, many things to do, many things to see. And yet, in such a spacious building, it appears the activity of choice was to go to the balconies and point. One wonders what was so interesting about those partaking of the tree—particularly for those who seemingly wanted nothing to do with it. Neal A. Maxwell remarked:

> "Why—really why—do disbelievers who line that spacious building watch so intently what the believers are doing? Surely there must be other things for the scorners to do—perhaps in the building's bowling alley—unless, deep within

their seeming disinterest, there is interest." (*Neal A. Maxwell Quote Book*, 295)

One of the most powerful sentences uttered by Lehi in this dream is "we heeded them not." Nephi explains why Lehi's sentence is so important—"as many as heeded them, had fallen away" (1 Nephi 8:34). Clearly, we *head* toward what we *heed.* The Lord warns that if we don't "give heed to the words of the prophets and apostles" we will be "cut off" (D&C 1:14). Jesus himself was subject to mists of darkness—he "suffered temptations but gave no heed unto them" (D&C 20:22). The issue of how we "heed not" the scoffers in the great and spacious building will be covered in more detail in the final chapters.

Applying the Dream to Our Reality

Dr. James Dobson, a Christian author and founder of Focus on the Family, described a hallway of doors, that interestingly, fits nicely into what might be inside a modern great and spacious building:

> Think of yourself as a teenager being required to walk alone down a long, dark corridor.

Low-wattage bulbs hang from the ceiling, casting eerie shadows on the walls. On either side of this hall are many large doors, each bearing a different inscription. They are called Alcohol, Marijuana, Hard Drugs, Pornography, Gambling, Homosexual Experimentation, Premarital Sex, Anorexia, and so on. Every form of addictive behavior is represented by at least one door. So there you are, groping along in the darkness and wondering what to do next. Should you stay on the straight and narrow—or push open one of the enticing doors? As you approach each portal, you can hear boisterous laughter and gaiety coming from within. Your friends—or people you want as friends—are already inside, and they are obviously having a blast. Every now and then you hear someone call your name and ask you to join the party. Who knows what excitement awaits those with the courage to enter? Slivers of light escaping from under each door reveal dancing bodies inside. Pounding music reverberates through the walls. As you stand there in the shadows, you ask yourself, "Why shouldn't I get in on the fun? Who has the right to shut me out?"

> That does it! You reach for the doorknob. What happens next could be remembered for a lifetime. Why? Because for a certain percentage of the individuals who open the doors, a tragedy begins to unfold. Lifelong addictions can be traced to that moment. (*Life on the Edge*, 189–90)

In Lehi's dream, a gulf divided the tree of life from the great and spacious building, but today, there seems to be no gulf at all. President Boyd K. Packer taught:

> Largely because of television, instead of looking over into the spacious building, we are, in effect, living inside of it. That is your fate in this generation. You are living in that great and spacious building. ("Lehi's Dream and You")

Is it possible to leave the building and join those at the tree? While that scenario is not addressed in the scriptures, we all know from experience that it's possible, in fact, it happens all the time. I remember one day sitting in priesthood meeting when a man in the back made a fascinating comment. I was fairly new in the ward, so his words were a bit of a shock to me—I never would have guessed! I scrambled to find a pencil and record what he said. He stood up and remarked, "Back when I was drinking and partying, I have to admit—I had a good time. I had a *great* time. I was in the great and spacious building and I was laughing at you guys. But then it turned on me. I lost my job, I lost my marriage, I lost the chance to raise my two daughters. And in 25 years, I spent $500,000 on drugs and alcohol."

Steve, the man who made this comment currently serves as a church service missionary, a powerful and loving force for good (tough=love, I should say) who, along with his wife, spends many hours at the local jail and prison teaching others how to find God and break their addictions. Interestingly, the teaching tool he uses most often (with members and non-members alike) is the metaphor of Lehi's Dream.

13

SEEING IT ALL AT ONCE

All of the elements of the dream have been presented and interpreted. Everything is in place. The tree, the building, the iron rod, and the mists of darkness have ascended from the ground. "Numberless concourses" of mankind have entered and divided themselves into the four groups Lehi saw. Now, we can imagine ourselves walking along with Lehi—what will we do?

President Boyd K. Packer said:

> You may think that Lehi's dream or vision has no special meaning for you, but it does. You are in it; all of us are in it. ("Finding Ourselves in Lehi's Dream," 22)

It's All about Agency

Picture in your mind each part of Lehi's dream; try to see it all at once. Look at the front cover of this book if needed. You are looking at a grand illustration of *agency*. In fact, the entire metaphor doesn't work unless there is agency. Agency is both wonderful and painful. The Lord taught, "Behold, here is the agency of man, and here is the condemnation of man" (D&C 93:31).

In order for us to freely choose the tree of life, choosing the great and spacious must also be an option. Forced abstinence is not the same as freely chosen virtue. Satan wanted equality of *outcome* ("I will redeem all mankind, that one soul shall not be lost" [Moses 4:1]). The Father's plan was for equality of *opportunity*. How did Satan propose to redeem everyone? Simple. Satan "sought to destroy the agency of man, which I, the Lord God, had given him" (Moses 4:3). By eliminating agency, he hoped to guarantee the outcome by limiting the opportunity. The Father's plan is to guarantee the opportunity, allowing individuals to exercise their own agency and choose the outcome. He will force no one to heaven. Again, Lehi's dream is a grand illustration of agency.

Some years after the vision, Lehi taught his son Jacob about "opposition in all things." In that same conversation, he added:

> Wherefore, men are free according to the flesh; and all things are given them which are expedient unto man. And they are free to choose liberty and eternal life, through the great Mediator of all men, or to choose captivity and death, according to the captivity and power of the devil; for he seeketh that all men might be miserable like unto himself. (2 Nephi 2:27)

"Choose you this day whom ye will serve," Joshua said, implying, of course, that there must be a choice (Joshua 24:15). In the world, as in Lehi's dream, there are many choices. From the tree of life on one end to the great and spacious building on the other, and every "strange road" and "forbidden path" in between. We are placed into this world with the power to choose and act, and that is the beginning of our test. The Savior said, "And we will prove them herewith, to see if they will do all things whatsoever the Lord their God shall command them" (Abraham 3:25).

Four Groups, Four Paths, Four Soils

As a result of agency, we symbolically see in Lehi's dream all of mankind dividing themselves into four groups. In fact, some have referred to Lehi's dream as "the parable of the paths" since there are four paths in which we find everyone divided (see McConkie and Millet, *Doctrinal Commentary on the Book of Mormon,* 1:57).

The Savior also divided all of the world into four groups in his parable of the sower, which has also been called "the parable of the four kinds of soil." Each of us can find ourselves in Lehi's dream, just as we can also find ourselves in Jesus' parable of the four different soils. Notice how the groups are similarly divided.

Recall that in the parable of the sower (see Matthew 13:3–8, 18–23) seeds fell upon four different kinds of soil, each of which brought forth different results. Jesus describes the spiritual readiness of all of mankind in that parable! Similarly, Lehi's dream describes all of mankind. This sobering fact is also an opportunity for us to ask ourselves, "Where am I in these parables?" and "Is this where I want to be?"

Lehi's Parable of the Four Paths *1 Nephi 8*	**Jesus' Parable of the Four Kinds of Soil** *Matthew 13*
Commenced in the path, overcome by mists, lost (23)	Among thorns, heard the word, care of the world choked the word, unfruitful (7, 22)
Partook, were ashamed, wandered off, were lost (25)	Stony places, received the word, endured for a while, by and by was offended (5, 20–21)
Partook, held fast, stayed (30)	Good ground, heard the word, understood it, brought forth fruit (8, 23)
No interest in the strait and narrow, moved directly toward the building (31, 32)	By the way side, wicked one caught away that which was sown (4, 19)

Personally, I believe these two parables are connected—and not just because they both divide mankind into four groups. When we look at Jesus' parable of the four kinds of soil and Lehi's parable of the four paths, I believe we are seeing different parts of a much larger story. One grand agricultural metaphor of soil, seed, season, and supper:

Part One: *The Soil.* Jesus sowed the seed, and the different responses men have to the seed are symbolized by four different types of soil. (See Matthew 13)

Part Two: *The Seed.* Alma the younger, encountered what we might call "good soil" among the poor of the Zoramites and persuaded them to plant the word (Christ) in their hearts so that it would grow. If it didn't grow, Alma said, it's because "your ground [or soil] is barren" (Alma 32:39), and the footnote directs us back to phase one—Matthew 13 and the parable of the sower, or four kinds of soil.

Part Three: *The Season.* Alma taught the Zoramites to nourish the seed with faith and patience so that it might have time to "take root" (Alma 32:42), and he indicated the type of plant he was teaching them to nourish when he warned, "if ye will not nourish the word . . . ye can never pluck of the fruit of the *tree of life*" (Alma 32:40; emphasis added).

Part Four: *The Supper.* Lehi partook of the fruit from the mature tree of life, and was shown his family's and all of mankind's various reactions to the tree in his dream (for a lengthier discussion, see the author's "Weed Your Brain, Grow Your Testimony").

THE TREE OF LIFE VERSUS THE GREAT AND SPACIOUS BUILDING

"Which came first, the chicken or the egg?" This ancient riddle has baffled elementary school science classes for years. In this context, we may ask, which came first, the tree or the seed? The tree came from a seed, which came from a tree, which came from a seed, and so forth back through eternity. The tree of life is an eternal symbol. We first read of the tree of life in Genesis 2, where God made the "tree of life [to grow] also in the midst of the garden" (Genesis 2:9). Lehi saw the tree of life in his dream, Alma the Younger referred to it, and we are promised that "to him that overcometh will I give to eat of the tree of life, which is in the midst of the paradise of God" (Revelation 2:7). Thus, the tree of life existed at the beginning of the creation story, in the middle of Lehi's dream, and in the paradise of God at the end of the world. *The tree is something God created or grew. The great and spacious building, by contrast, is temporary, man-made, and will eventually fall* as Nephi testified (1 Nephi 11:36). The tree is spiritual and the building is secular. The contrast could not be greater.

Obviously, the place where we want to be, and where we want to remain, is near the tree of life. And yet, we are commanded to go "into all the world" and preach the gospel to every creature. This is a bit of a paradox—we are counseled to "stand . . . in holy places, and be not moved" (D&C 87:8) but also to "go into all the world." Jesus clarified when asked the Father, "I pray not that thou shouldest take them out of the world, but that thou shouldest keep them from the evil" (John 17:15). The phrase "be in the world but not of the world" is a restatement of Jesus' prayer.

In Lehi's dream, we stay near the tree. But in life,

we go out into all the world and preach the gospel to every creature, even knocking on the doors of residents of the great and spacious building. So it is vital that we take the tree *with us* wherever we go, and that is exactly what the scriptures promise us is possible. Alma assured the Zoramites that if they would plant the word in their hearts, and maintain it through a season of growth, it would "become a tree, springing up *in you* unto everlasting life" (Alma 33:23, emphasis added). Thus, the tree of life is portable, and it can be "in you" or in us as we go out into the world. The tree of life is a symbol of Christ, and we are promised each week at the sacrament table that we can "always have his Spirit to be with [us]" (Moroni 4:3) as we live in the world.

The great and spacious building is nothing but one giant distraction. It is large enough to distract our eyes and loud enough to distract our ears. It is modern and spacious and has more glitz and glamour than a simple tree. I suppose it had some measure of glory too, but it was temporary—a glory Hugh Nibley described very well:

> Imitation glory is darkness; it's sad. The glory of a merry-go-round, or the glory of Las Vegas, all

> that light, all that neon glitter. Is that your idea of glory? That's not very glorious. It's the opposite; it's very sad, isn't it. (*Ancient Documents and the Pearl of Great Price*)

Personally, I believe there were things to eat in the great and spacious building too, but nothing on the menu with the soul-satisfying power of the fruit at the tree of life. I suppose the dining experience in the great and spacious is described perfectly by Isaiah:

> It shall be unto them, even as unto a hungry man which dreameth, and behold he eateth but he awaketh and his soul is empty; or like unto a thirsty man which dreameth, and behold he drinketh but he awaketh and behold he is faint, and his soul hath appetite; yea, even so shall the multitude of all the nations be that fight against Mount Zion. (2 Nephi 27:3)

It is spacious, so there must be a lot of room inside. Even though, as mentioned earlier, the activity of choice seems to be mocking and jeering. But every activity is just another distraction from the only activity that really matters.

One right thing to do, and a number of "fruitless" things to do. There is one way to live the "plan of happiness" and a thousand ways to live the "plan of misery." To paraphrase William Law, "Unless you have chosen the kingdom of God first, in the end it will make no difference what you have chosen instead" (in Maxwell, *The Smallest Part*, iv). So it really makes no difference what all those spacious halls contained.

Nephi saw everything his father Lehi saw, but all of the symbols were intertwined with the life of Christ. After Nephi saw the more sobering and troubling events in the life of the Savior—events such as the trial and crucifixion and the multitudes of the earth gathered together to fight against the twelve apostles—he beheld the great and spacious building. In this case, the angel himself gives the interpretation: "Behold the world and the wisdom thereof" (1 Nephi 11:35). In the next chapter, the angel adds, "And the large and spacious building, which thy father saw, is vain imaginations and the pride of the children of men" (1 Nephi 12:18).

Nephi also added a couple of descriptors to the

interpretation: "I saw and bear record, that the great and spacious building was the pride of the world; and it fell, and the fall thereof was exceedingly great. And the angel of the Lord spake unto me again saying: Thus shall be the destruction of all nations, kindreds, tongues, and people, that shall fight against the twelve apostles of the Lamb" (1 Nephi 11:36).

The Fountain of Living Water versus the Fountain of Filthy Water

The water in Lehi's dream doesn't get as much attention as the other elements, perhaps because their descriptions are a little bit confusing. There is a fountain near the tree, but there is also a filthy river in which people drown. Are they two different rivers, or different ends of the same river? A careful reading of three different witnesses across three different chapters reveals the answer:

Lehi: I beheld a *river of water;* and it ran along, and it was near the tree of which I was partaking the fruit (1 Nephi 8:13; emphasis added).

Lehi: And it came to pass that many were *drowned*

in the depths of the fountain; and many were lost from his view, wandering in strange roads (1 Nephi 8:32; emphasis added).

Nephi: I beheld that the rod of iron, which my father had seen, was the word of God, which led to the *fountain of living waters,* or to the tree of life; *which waters are a representation of the love of God* (1 Nephi 11:25; emphasis added).

The Angel: And the angel spake unto me, saying: Behold the *fountain of filthy water* which thy father saw; yea, even the river of which he spake; and *the depths thereof are the depths of hell* (1 Nephi 12:16; emphasis added).

Nephi: And I said unto them that *the water which my father saw was filthiness;* and so much was his mind swallowed up in other things that he beheld not the filthiness of the water (1 Nephi 15:27; emphasis added).

These verses seem to describe two fountains or rivers: A fountain of living waters, representing the love of God, and a fountain of filthy water, which is the depths of hell. These fountains and their symbolic importance are more than just a side note; they are a testimony of the reality of opposition in all things. Bruce Satterfield observed:

> Lehi must have been able to see that everything the Lord established had its opposite. The tree which brought eternal life to all who endured in partaking of the fruit was opposed by the great and spacious building which brought destruction to all who dwelt therein. The living waters which brought the sweetness of life was opposed by the river of filthy water which brought the depths of hell. The rod of iron and the strait and narrow path which led those who entered therein to the tree was opposed by the mist of darkness which caused those who let go of the rod to wander off the path to their destruction. ("Lehi's Dream")

Although the people in the dream can be divided into four groups, we must be preoccupied with the one group—the group we must find ourselves in. The group who partakes of the tree of life and stays. Everything else is a distraction.

Feeling Joy versus Feeling Ashamed

Lehi's dream may be described as a battle of feelings. Feeling the love of God, the joy of partaking of the fruit of the tree of life, versus the feelings of being ashamed, and the desire to conform with the pride, the vain imaginations, and the wisdom of the world. For some, feeling the joy of eating at the tree of life gave them the desire to stay at any cost. For others, feeling the disapproval from the world was just too much, and they wandered away.

Many investigators of the restored gospel would prefer to see the gold plates than go to all the trouble to gain a testimony and "feel" in their hearts that the record is true.

The world says "seeing is believing," and—let's be honest—who wouldn't *love* to see an angel? Many of us might also prefer the "seeing" method for discerning and confirming truth. One of the steps of the scientific method is to "observe the data." With what? With our eyes. We say, "show me, let me see it with my own eyes."

The Lord, however, seems to prefer guiding his

children by sending us feelings. He wants us to walk by faith, not by sight (see 2 Corinthians 5:7). He works more by the formula "believing is seeing." The Lord promises that when we ask in faith we may "feel that it is right" (D&C 9:8). He doesn't say, "now that you've *seen*, you will have *faith*." Rather, "because of thy *faith* thou hast *seen* . . ." (Ether 3:9; emphasis added).

In Lehi's dream, sojourners suddenly lose their ability to see, and must "feel" their way toward the tree of life by holding fast to the iron rod. Most of us seek to feel the truth of the gospel. But if we don't already believe with our hearts, we are unlikely to believe with our eyes. Joseph Fielding McConkie has written:

> All true religion centers in feelings, and since feelings are not subject to a system of weights and measures, it is difficult to describe them to the unspiritual. Again, our inability to describe those feelings doesn't negate their reality. An infant's inability to sense and feel the reality of parental love is not conditioned on his ability to explain those feelings. To know truth by sense and feeling without being able to explain or rationally

> defend it is an experience common to all mankind. (*Seeking the Spirit*, 8)

After Joseph Smith translated the golden plates, they were returned to Moroni. "How convenient," the critics say, who must see something with their eyes in order to prove its existence. Suppose we were suddenly able to show people the plates. Do you think their presence would create instant believers? Not likely. What would be created would be a hundred theories about how someone had made a counterfeit set.

What would happen if the Lord showed us things that we could see with our eyes? Would unbelievers be convinced? Interestingly, Laman and Lemuel *did* see miraculous things. What happened to them? They didn't believe their own eyes. In fact, they accused Nephi of tricking them. They said, Nephi "worketh many things by his cunning arts, that he may deceive our eyes . . ." (1 Nephi 16:38). "Show me, show me, show me!" some say, "I will believe it when I see it with my own eyes." So the Lord shows them, and they say, "I don't believe my eyes!" No wonder the Lord prefers to work by the "believing is seeing" method.

Those in the great and spacious building could obviously see from afar the tree of life, a glorious symbol of Christ! But it did them no good. It was impossible for them to know from such a distance the feelings that came to those who were partaking. They could not know, by sight alone, that the fruit filled those who partook with great joy. Similarly, many saw Jesus Christ during his mortal ministry. But they were past feeling, and never gained a testimony of who he was.

The great and spacious building also drew people to it because of feelings. Feeling embarrassed, feeling ashamed, feeling foolish caused many to leave the tree of life, and instead "feel their way" to the great and spacious building. There they were welcomed and felt safe in conforming with everyone else who was pointing and mocking. There they were immersed in the unrighteous feelings of pride and worldly wisdom. Popular opinion won.

Meanwhile, across the way, multitudes were partaking of the greatest joy available—and although those in the building could *see* what was happening across the way, they couldn't *feel* a thing. It reminds me of a poster

I saw once depicting a hobo dancing by the train tracks with the caption: "Those who danced were thought to be quite insane by those who could not hear the music." In this case, those who partook were thought to be quite insane by those who could not taste or feel what those at the tree were tasting and feeling. And instead of wondering, *What's going on over there?* in their pride, they simply decided that whatever those tree partakers are doing, it can't possibly be as much fun as what we're doing, and they decided to mock.

14

OVERHEARD FROM THE GREAT AND SPACIOUS

We are given only three phrases to describe what the residents of the great and spacious building were doing: "mocking," "pointing their fingers," and "scoffing," but that's about it. I've always wanted to know, what *exactly* were they saying? Why did their taunts have such power? What could they possibly say that would be so persuasive that it would lure believers away from the tree of life, and away from the fruit that was most sweet, most delicious, and most joyous to the soul? I believe we can look to the rest of the Book of Mormon for some answers. President Ezra Taft Benson taught:

> The Book of Mormon exposes the enemies of Christ. It confounds false doctrines and lays down contention (see 1 Nephi 3:12). It fortifies

> the humble followers of Christ against the evil designs, strategies, and doctrines of the devil in our day. The type of apostates in the Book of Mormon are similar to the type we have today. God, with His infinite foreknowledge, so molded the Book of Mormon that we might see the error and know how to combat false educational, political, religious, and philosophical concepts of our time. (*The Teachings of Ezra Taft Benson*, 56)

Since the type of apostates in Lehi's time are the same type we have today, we can make some educated guesses about what the scoffers were actually saying. John Welch taught:

> Lehi's vision of the great and spacious building, for example, tells us graphically that the one main weapon used by the wicked is mocking and derision. I don't think we guard ourselves enough against behaving this way. Yet when you know your opponent's playbook, it's a lot easier to plan your defense. No better exposé of the cunning but rakish ways of the devil can be found than in the Book of Mormon. ("Study, Faith, and the Book of Mormon," 22)

President James E. Faust spoke of the variety of messages we may overhear while near the great and spacious building when he taught:

> The adversary tries to smother this voice with a multitude of loud, persistent, persuasive, and appealing voices:
>
> - Murmuring voices that conjure up perceived injustices.
> - Whining voices that abhor challenge and work.
> - Seductive voices offering sensual enticements.
> - Soothing voices that lull us into carnal security.
> - Intellectual voices that profess sophistication and scholarly superiority.
> - Proud voices that rely on the arm of flesh.
> - Flattering voices that puff us up with pride.
> - Cynical voices that destroy hope.
> - Entertaining voices that promote pleasure seeking.
> - Commercial voices that tempt us to "spend money for that which is of no worth" and to "labor for that which cannot satisfy" (2 Nephi 9:51).
> - Delirious voices that spawn the desire for a

> "high." I refer not to a drug- or alcohol-induced high but rather a high obtained by pursuing dangerous, death-defying experiences for nothing more than a thrill. Life, even our own, is so precious that we are accountable to the Lord for it, and we should not trifle with it. (*Finding Light in a Dark World*, 99)

While there are probably hundreds of different taunts and objections being hurled from the great and spacious building at the partakers, we'll discuss only seven:

- "There is no God"
- "There is a God, but he doesn't care what we do"
- "God is Love, so he doesn't punish people"
- "We don't believe in organized religion"
- "You think you're better than us"
- "Why are you trying to convert people?"
- "There is a God, but you are an overzealous fanatic" (from other church members)

There Is No God, and You Are Foolish

Korihor was an antichrist who denied the existence of God. But don't think for a minute that his efforts stopped there. Korihor never said, "This is what I think, but you can believe whatever you want." No, no, no. He, along with other occupants of the great and spacious building, was not content to live his own beliefs and let others do as they wished. He attacked believers by characterizing them as:

Bound (you have no freedom!)
Foolish (you are stupid!)
Yoked (you are controlled by others!)
Frenzied (you are not all there!)
Deranged (you are insane!) (See Alma 30:13, 16)

Korihor accused the religious leaders of keeping people from enjoying their "rights and privileges" (Alma 30:27). What he meant by rights and privileges was that they should eat, drink, and be merry, and much worse. Korihor taught that "whatsoever a man did was no crime" (Alma 30:17). In other words, since nothing is wrong, everything is right. Finally, he declared that "when a man [is] dead, that [is] the end thereof" (Alma 30:18), which would mean there is no judgment, no afterlife, no consequences, and no accountability.

The impact of Korihor's philosophy was that it led "many women, and also men, to commit whoredoms" (Alma 30:18). Among the so-called rights and privileges he was talking about were the rights and privileges to sin, to behave immorally, and to break the law of chastity. We can only imagine the sorrowful aftermath of that behavior for the men and women who followed Korihor in enjoying their rights and privileges. Broken hearts, broken homes, regret, remorse, and a lingering legacy of sorrow and hurt for families. Sin doesn't do anyone any good, even if it isn't believed to be a sin at the time.

Today, atheist organizations are buying billboard space to promote their nonbelief while condemning others' beliefs with great zeal. Like Korihor, they are not content with simply living their own beliefs, just as occupants in the great and spacious building were not content to stay inside their spacious abode. Their preoccupation was with believers. We live in a free society, so we will continue to hear these messages and many others, and that's as expected. We use that same freedom to share the gospel. We just have to be prepared for the attacks we hear, and be able to identify their source. Lehi's dream helps us do just that.

Korihor told the believers they were "bound" and "yoked" by their beliefs, and today, our members, especially our youth are often told, "You can't do *anything* in your church!" Actually, we have as much freedom as everyone else, but with that freedom, we choose to follow God—a God who loves us so much that he desires to protect us from consequences, or as Jacob said, the "awful consequences" of sin (Jacob 3:12). We are free to choose our actions, but not the consequences of our actions.

So, if a voice in your life shouts or whispers, "there is no God," you know where it is coming from. Something about partaking of the fruit of the tree of life is bothersome to those in the great and spacious, so they seek to "interrupt [your] rejoicings" (Alma 30:22).

There Is a God, but He Doesn't Care What We Do

Some teach that God is not really concerned with our behavior. One such character was Nehor:

> And he also testified unto the people that all mankind should be saved at the last day, and that they need not fear nor tremble, but that they might lift up their heads and rejoice; for the Lord had created all men, and had also redeemed all men; and, in the end, all men should have eternal life. (Alma 1:4)

Nehor believed that the teachers of the gospel should be "popular," meaning they should be supported by the population, and that if you liked their preaching, you should support them with your money. Many liked Nehor's ideas, and even after he was gone, his philosophy lived on for a time until the end of Ammonihah and the "Desolation of Nehors" when many of his followers were wiped out in one day (see Alma 16:11).

Which leads us to an interesting question—why in the world would the compilers and abridgers of the Book of Mormon give any written space at all to Korihor and Nehor? Why should any of their false teachings be published? Clearly, the inspired men who gave us the record wanted latter-day readers to know that when we hear of some clever, new religious philosophy, we will know that it's really nothing new at all;

it's just another way to avoid or "transcend" true devotion, consecration, and obedience. To be sure, what Nehor taught has a certain appeal, especially if you're into something for nothing. Robert Eaton wrote:

> The fallacy of such a doctrine, of course, is that it incorrectly asserts that salvation is guaranteed for all and that how we live, what we believe, and whether we repent are completely irrelevant, which ideas are of course blatantly false. . . . Nehor had discovered something practiced by religious opportunists since the beginning: that preachers who tell people what they want to hear not only become popular but can get listeners to support them financially. (*Digging Deeper,* 128)

Is this a new idea? Teaching people what they want to hear? Well, if 740 B.C. is new, then I guess you could call it new. Isaiah saw this tendency in the people when he taught:

> This is a rebellious people, lying children, children that will not hear the law of the Lord: Which say to the seers, See not; and to the prophets, Prophesy not unto us right things,

> speak unto us smooth things, prophesy deceits. (Isaiah 30:9–10)

Nephi explicitly warned us that the Book of Mormon would come forth in a day when people would teach that God wasn't that interested in justice, or that he would look upon sin with a degree of allowance:

> And there shall also be many which shall say: Eat, drink, and be merry; nevertheless, fear God—he will justify in committing a little sin; yea, lie a little, take the advantage of one because of his words, dig a pit for thy neighbor; there is no harm in this; and do all these things, for tomorrow we die; and if it so be that we are guilty, God will beat us with a few stripes, and at last we shall be saved in the kingdom of God. (2 Nephi 28:8)

Not only does God care about what we do, but he cares about us. What we do is what we become, and he wants us to become like him. So when the voices in your life mock you for trying to be like Jesus, remember that Jesus too endured mocking voices even when he was suffering upon the cross.

God Is Love, So He Doesn't Punish People

Elder Dallin H. Oaks observed, "Some seem to value God's love because of their hope that His love is so great and so unconditional that it will mercifully excuse them from obeying His laws" ("Love and Law," 26).

Alma the Younger spent time teaching each of his sons, and we have his words. He taught his son Helaman in Alma 36 and 37. He taught Shiblon in Alma 38. Corianton had some doctrinal misunderstandings, which may have led to his behavioral problems, so he got chapters 39 through 42. President Boyd K. Packer taught that:

> True doctrine, understood, changes attitudes and behavior. The study of the doctrines of the gospel will improve behavior quicker than a study of behavior will improve behavior. (*Mine Errand from the Lord*, 307)

Perhaps the story of Corianton is preserved to help those in our day who may have similar misunderstandings. For example, among the many concerns that

Alma perceived worried his son, he addressed the justice of God.

> And now, my son, I perceive there is somewhat more which doth worry your mind, which ye cannot understand—which is concerning the justice of God in the punishment of the sinner; for ye do try to suppose that it is injustice that the sinner should be consigned to a state of misery. (Alma 42:1)

Many in our day may have a similar confusion. If God is so loving, why does he punish his children? To answer this question, Alma taught Corianton about Adam and Eve's fall, and how it was brought about by their own disobedience. Yes, it would be unjust to assign souls to misery if they were sinless, but each of us sins. Gerald N. Lund taught that following the fall of Adam comes the "fall of me" (*Jesus Christ: Key to the Plan of Salvation*, 95). Thus, each of us is a sinner, and we have brought upon ourselves the justice of God by our own disobedience. We don't worship a God who loves to punish his children, but a God who delights to bless us. He is a just God, but also a God of mercy. And because of his mercy, we are given time, a "probationary state," a window in which we can repent so that justice and mercy can be satisfied.

Make no mistake about it, God is loving. That's why he extends mercy to appease the demands of justice. He loves us so much that sometimes he says those three little words—not "I love you," but "thou shalt not." The commandments God gives us are not to keep us from enjoying our rights and privileges, but to help us avoid the awful consequences of sin. Viewed this way, we can understand why the hymn says, "How gentle God's commands! How kind his precepts are" (*Hymns,* no. 125). God's commandments are evidence of his love for us.

Sometimes we say that keeping the commandments will help us to live *with* God again—which is true, but incomplete. We are not only hoping to live with God, but to live *like* God. The commandments, the standards, and our emphasis on doing good works are not so that we can *earn* heaven, but so that we can *learn* heaven (see Brad Wilcox, *Learning [Not Earning] Heaven*). The Atonement of Christ makes it possible to live with God, and Christ works upon our hearts that we might learn to live *like* God.

We Don't Believe in Organized Religion

A recent *Deseret News* article by Jerry Earl Johnston mentioned "Designer Faith," while commenting on the trend toward personalized, individual approaches to spirituality. The idea is that individuals can choose their own beliefs as if they were in line at a buffet. "*I'll have some 'love one another' and some 'judge not,' and that's all I want in my belief. I don't want any of those commandments or ordinances or expectations about Christian behavior.*" We can certainly understand the appeal, but shouldn't we be wondering what God wants us to believe, not just what feels most comfortable or easiest for each individual to believe?

Another phrase gaining popularity is "I'm spiritual, but not religious." Or, in other words, I don't believe in "organized religion." It's easy to take shots at organized religion. The major denominations are highly visible, they're perceived to be wealthy, and you can find adherents who belong to major denominations who are not perfect. And when one of them steps out of line, it makes the headlines. "Aha!" people conclude. "Organized religion is just a bunch of hypocrites." Well, that's true in the sense that none of our actions match the level of our beliefs. We all mess up. I like how Zig Ziglar responded to someone who said they wouldn't come to his church because it was filled with hypocrites. "That's okay," Zig said, "we've got room for one more" (see *See You at the Top*, 69).

As a bishop, I once announced that we moved the records of all the perfect people out of the ward, so it was just us imperfect folks who comprised the congregation. That way, they wouldn't be shocked when someone in the ward, including the leadership, didn't live up to their expectations.

The argument for organized religion goes all the way back to Jesus. Not everyone believes that Jesus organized a church, but we do. He called apostles and ordained them. He gave them priesthood and conferred keys to govern the Church. The Church is where we go because it is where the priesthood is, and where the ordinances of salvation are. It's also a wonderful place to meet with each other and talk to one another concerning the welfare of our souls (see Moroni 6:5).

While practicing our faith is a highly personal matter, we might briefly consider one of the blessings of organized religion for just two of its key purposes—to love our neighbor and to take care of the poor. Like other organized religions, our church sends relief supplies around the globe following earthquakes, tsunamis, hurricanes, and other natural disasters. If there were 14 million of us each with our own individual "designer faith," who would send the trucks? Who would organize the relief? How would those in trouble receive the help they need?

You Think You're Better Than Us!

I once had lunch with a friend who surprised me when he announced he was a vegetarian. I must admit it, I was uncomfortable. I kept wondering if he was looking down on me because I chose to eat a hamburger. It was a great lesson for me, because it taught me how others might feel in my presence when they discover I don't drink or smoke or curse and that I try to keep a multitude of other commandments. It was easy for my mind to jump to the conclusion, "Well, since you don't eat meat and I do, you probably think I'm an evil, bad sinner." My lunch appointment on that day taught me how easy it would be to assume that others are condemning me because they have a different set of beliefs, even though that might not be true at all! (It also taught me that veggie-burgers have a long way to go).

How can we help people not feel uncomfortable around us as we attempt to live our beliefs? One way is to internalize the wisdom President Dieter F. Uchtdorf saw captured on a bumper sticker:

> "Don't judge me because I sin differently than you." We must recognize that we are all imperfect—that we are beggars before God. Haven't we all, at one time or another, meekly approached the mercy seat and pleaded for grace? Haven't we wished with all the energy of our souls for mercy—to be forgiven for the mistakes we have made and the sins we have committed? Because we all depend on the mercy of God, how can we deny to others any measure of the grace we

> so desperately desire for ourselves? My beloved brothers and sisters, should we not forgive as we wish to be forgiven? ("The Merciful Obtain Mercy," 75)

Personally, I know I have nothing to feel superior about, because during my lifetime, I've thought things I shouldn't have thought, I've said things I shouldn't have said, and I've done things I shouldn't have done. To put it another way, "I ain't got nothin' on nobody."

I've noticed that there is danger in spending all this time writing about those "publicans and sinners" over there in the great and spacious building. If our spot near the tree of life becomes a Rameumptom where we congratulate each other on our chosen-ness and look down on everyone else, then we're occupying nothing more than a branch office of the great and spacious.

Even when we are aware of our own imperfections and are well aware that we need the Savior's forgiveness as much as anyone, we might still hear the claim, "you think you're better than us." In those cases, there is not much to do except to answer that we all need God, and that he is reaching out to all of us. Elder

Robert D. Hales taught us how to respond when he taught, "We love them. Whatever their race, creed, religion, or political persuasion, if we follow Christ and show forth His courage, we must love them. We do not feel we are *better than* they are. Rather, we desire with our love to show them a *better way*—the way of Jesus Christ" ("Christian Courage," 75). We may never be able to convince the inconvincible, but we must never cease to labor (see Moroni 9:6). All we can do is all we can do. Moroni worried that the Gentiles would mock at his words, and the Lord told Moroni (and all of us) not to worry about what others think:

> If they have not charity it mattereth not unto thee, thou hast been faithful; wherefore, thy garments shall be made clean. And because thou hast seen thy weakness thou shalt be made strong. (Ether 12:37)

Our concern should be about what would prevent us from "seeing our weakness," and that would be pride, which is characterized by the great and spacious building.

Have you ever had someone try to bait you with

the question "Do you think I'm going to hell?" My favorite answer is, "How in the world should I know?"

Elder Dallin H. Oaks once gave a very helpful talk in which he made a distinction between "intermediate judgments" and "final judgments." Intermediate judgments we must make, but we must make carefully as we choose our path in life, as we choose someone to marry, someone to tend our children, etc. Final judgments are the ones God has forbidden us to make. Elder Oaks concluded:

> We should refrain from anything that seems to be a final judgment of any person—manifesting our determination to leave final judgments to the Lord, who alone has the capacity to judge.
>
> In the intermediate judgments we must make, we should take care to judge righteously. We should seek the guidance of the Spirit in our decisions. We should limit our judgments to our own stewardships. Whenever possible we should refrain from judging people until we have an adequate knowledge of the facts. So far as possible, we should judge circumstances rather than people. In all our judgments we should apply

righteous standards. And, in all of this, we must remember the command to forgive. ("Judge Not and Judging," 180)

Why Are You Trying to Convert People?

Some from the great and spacious might say, why don't you just keep your religion to yourself? (Even though they can't seem to leave the tree-of-life partakers alone.)

Article of Faith 11 says that we claim the privilege of worshiping the Almighty God according to the dictates of our own conscience, and allow all men the same privilege to worship how, where, or what they may. However, we send missionaries all over the world. Why? Because coupled with our belief in letting others worship however they choose is the Savior's directive: "Go ye therefore, and teach all nations, baptizing them in the name of the Father, and of the Son, and of the Holy Ghost" (Matthew 28:19). Will everyone believe what we teach? No, but the Savior asks us to teach all nations notwithstanding.

The Prophet Joseph Smith said, "We don't ask

any people to throw away any good they have got; we only ask them to come and get more" (*Teachings*, 275). Similarly, President Gordon B. Hinckley taught, "Let me say that we appreciate the truth in all churches and the good which they do. We say to the people, in effect, you bring with you all the good that you have, and then let us see if we can add to it. That is the spirit of this work. That is the essence of our missionary service" ("Messages of Inspiration").

There Is a God, but You Are an Overzealous Fanatic (from Church Members)

Is it possible that some of us might be acting like residents of the great and spacious but not realize it? It's sad when a missionary comes home, and friends want him to hurry up and adjust or get back to normal. "Get off your mission already!" they say, if he is still interested in studying his scriptures or making gospel study a permanent part of his routine. If "getting back to normal" means getting more comfortable with sin or mediocrity, that's not a worthy goal. Boyd K. Packer taught an unfortunate truth when he declared:

> You who are young will see many things that will try your courage and test your faith. All of the mocking does not come from outside of the Church. Let me say that again: All of the mocking does not come from outside of the Church. ("Lehi's Dream and You")

Some might say, even from within the Church, that you have to be "balanced." That you can't be a Sammy Seminary or a Molly Mormon all your life. Balance is an interesting word. In many ways, we do want to be balanced, for instance, when it comes to work and play, when it comes to spending time at work or at home, or dividing attention between our Church calling and our family. But if we're talking about striking a balance between righteousness and wickedness, that's not what we're after. That's not balance. That's being lukewarm. Imagine the absurdity, "I want to be 50 percent righteous and 50 percent wicked so that I can be a balanced, well-rounded person."

Elder Carlos E. Asay spoke of "a vicious lie," vicious

perhaps because it was not shouted from the great and spacious, but repeated in the Church:

> There is a lie—a vicious lie—circulating among the Latter-day Saints and taking its toll among the young. It is that a "balanced man" is one who deliberately guards against becoming too righteous. This lie would have you believe that it is possible to live happily and successfully . . . with one foot in Babylon and one foot in Zion. ("Be Men!" 41)

When Nephi was given his own view of his father's dream, he saw something startling:

> And the multitude of the earth was gathered together; and I beheld that they were in a large and spacious building, like unto the building which my father saw. And the angel of the Lord spake unto me again, saying: Behold the world and the wisdom thereof; yea, behold the *house of Israel* hath gathered together to fight against the twelve apostles of the Lamb. (1 Nephi 11:35; emphasis added)

Sadly, Nephi saw that it was the house of Israel,

the Lord's chosen people who were fighting against the twelve apostles. We are also the house of Israel living in the latter-days. Whose side are we on? Blaine Yorgason related this sad story:

> A close friend of mine is striving to bring his life more in line with the doctrines of Christ so he will be better able to deal with these calamitous times. Recently he had a sad confrontation with some members of his family. These were "active" Latter-day Saints, by the way, good people whom he loved. Yet when he tried to explain to them what had become important to him, what really mattered, he discovered that they had grown complacent or outright scornful of spiritual issues. They scoffed when he spoke to them of receiving a little personal revelation through the power of the Holy Ghost, and they laughingly referred to him as an extremist, a fanatic, one who couldn't keep both feet in the real world. "As if I really wanted to," my friend added in his letter describing these events to me. He then pointed out to them that when the angel showed Nephi the great and spacious building (the pride and wisdom of

> the world), it was peopled to a great extent by the house of Israel (modern Church members), who had "gathered together to fight against the twelve apostles of the Lamb" (1 Nephi 11:35). "Are these people you?" he asked his loved ones. "Are you the scoffers and the scorners and the simply complacent?" (*Spiritual Progression in the Last Days*, 10–11)

I suppose there are as many falsehoods coming from the great and spacious building as there are occupants, so it's impossible to identify everything that they are saying or that they may say in the future. Perhaps that is why Lehi didn't tell us exactly what their words were, only that they were scoffing, mocking, and pointing their fingers. One thing is certain—the voices will continue.

What is less certain is what we will do. Of the many voices which call to us from the great and spacious building, there is a quiet voice, a voice that is not loud, not harsh, but which pierces to our very center (see 3 Nephi 11:3). It's difficult to filter out all the noise, but it's possible if we focus on what is real and lasting—feasting on the fruit of the tree of life, which is sweet above all that is sweet, pure above all that is pure, and most joyous to the soul.

15

BUT WE HEEDED THEM NOT: NOT SO SIMPLE ANYMORE

How did Lehi and his family react to the mocking, scoffing, and pointing fingers from the great and spacious building? One simple sentence, "We heeded them not" (1 Nephi 8:33).

According to the 1828 Webster's Dictionary, "heed" means "to mind; to regard with care; to take notice of; to attend to; to observe" (in Largey, *The Book of Mormon Reference Companion,* 832).

So, in one sense, if heed means "to mind," as in, "you mind your grandma today," it would mean to obey. So perhaps we "heed not" the words coming from the great and spacious by not obeying what they're telling us to do. If "heeding them not" means simply ignoring them, that's another problem. Perhaps it was easier for the individuals in Lehi's dream to "heed them not." After all, there was a great and terrible gulf dividing the building from the tree of life (1 Nephi 12:18). Today, the taunters are in our face. They are in our schools. They are on our airwaves. Sometimes they are in our families. President Packer has said more than once that we are raising our children in enemy territory (see "Counsel to Youth," 16–18).

As mentioned earlier, he also observed that we are now living *in* the great and spacious building so "heeding them not" is not as easy as simply turning away, since we're tenants at the same address! The lifestyles of the great and spacious are the lifestyles our families are surrounded by, and this time, we can't escape by sailing across the oceans or crossing the plains. Elder Jeffrey R. Holland observed:

> The Church of God will never again flee. It will never again leave Ur in order to leave Haran, in order to leave Canaan, in order to leave Jerusalem, in order to leave England, in order to leave Kirtland, in order to leave Nauvoo, in order to go who knows where. No, as Brigham Young said for us all, "We have been kicked out of the

frying-pan into the fire, out of the fire into the middle of the floor, and here we are and here we will stay." ("Israel, Israel, God Is Calling")

At times, we *must* respond to the voices from the great and spacious building, so the question is, How? I will use as a resource three talks from modern-day apostles, Elders Robert D. Hales, M. Russell Ballard, and Jeffrey R. Holland, to try to answer that question.

Help Others Understand Truth

In a powerful address called "Christian Courage," Elder Robert D. Hales taught:

> *As true disciples, our primary concern must be others' welfare, not personal vindication.* Questions and criticisms give us an opportunity to reach out to others and demonstrate that they matter to our Heavenly Father and to us. Our aim should be to help them understand the truth, not defend our egos or score points in a theological debate. Our heartfelt testimonies are the most powerful answer we can give our accusers. And such testimonies can only be borne in love and meekness.

> We should be like Edward Partridge, of whom the Lord said, "His heart is pure before me, for he is like unto Nathanael of old, in whom there is no guile" (D&C 41:11). To be guileless is to have a childlike innocence, to be slow to take offense and quick to forgive. ("Christian Courage," 73–74)

Sister Elaine S. Dalton, general Young Women president, told of one young man, a student body officer at a large university, who found himself in a massive peer-pressure situation while attending a leadership conference in Chicago. During a get-to-know-you game, trees in a courtyard were labeled, "strongly agree," "partially agree," "strongly disagree," and "mildly disagree," and participants were asked to run to the tree whose label reflected their viewpoint on certain issues as they were announced.

> Toward the end of this exercise, the leader asked, "Do you believe in premarital sex?" Without hesitation, this young man ran to the tree marked "strongly disagree." To his amazement, he was the only one there! All the other student leaders were laughing and pointing at

> him and saying, "Oh, Jess, you are so funny. We all know you're not really serious." At that moment Jess said he knew exactly what he must do and so he loudly declared, "I'm not funny. I'm serious!" There was a stunned silence, and then the group dispersed, leaving Jess standing alone by the tree. He felt out of place and, yes, weird. But he wasn't weird. He was right. And he was not alone. During the week, many of the student leaders came to him privately and said that they wished they had known years earlier what he knew. Jess later said, "It was easy because I knew that I represented not only the university but my family, the Church, and the Savior." ("At All Times, in All Things, and in All Places," 116–17)

Can you picture the critical moment for this young man in your mind? There he is, *standing alone by a tree, while others are laughing and pointing.* Remind you of anything? Jess's simple but heartfelt testimony shared with Christian courage had an impact on others who were participating, to the point that they sought him out privately to share respect for his point of view.

Elder Hales also suggested that we must be guided

by the Holy Ghost who will help us adapt our responses according to the situation:

> To respond in a Christlike way cannot be scripted or based on a formula. The Savior responded differently in every situation. When He was confronted by wicked King Herod, He remained silent. When He stood before Pilate, He bore a simple and powerful testimony of His divinity and purpose. Facing the money-changers who were defiling the temple, He exercised His divine responsibility to preserve and protect that which was sacred. Lifted up upon a cross, He uttered the incomparable Christian response: "Father, forgive them; for they know not what they do" (Luke 23:34). ("Christian Courage," 72)

Suppose, for example, our children are taking a pounding at school about their stand on social issues regarding marriage and family. Don't others have agency? Are we forcing our views on them? Are we being judgmental when we define what marriage should be for everyone? Jeffrey R. Holland addressed this very issue:

In those situations you are going to have to explain sensitively why some principles are defended and some sins opposed wherever they are found because the issues and the laws involved are not just social or political but eternal in their consequence. And while not wishing to offend those who believe differently from us, we are even more anxious not to offend God, or as the scripture says, "not offend him who is your lawgiver" (D&C 64:13)—and I am speaking here of serious moral laws.

But to make the point, let me use the example of a lesser law. It is a little like a teenager saying, "Now that I can drive, I know I am supposed to stop at a red light, but do we really have to be judgmental and try to get everyone else to stop at red lights? Does everyone have to do what we do? Don't others have their agency? Must they behave as we do?" You then have to explain why, yes, we do hope all will stop at a red light. And you have to do this without demeaning those who transgress or who believe differently than we believe because, yes, they do have their moral agency.

> My young friends, there is a wide variety of beliefs in this world, and there is moral agency for all, but no one is entitled to act as if God is mute on these subjects or as if commandments only matter if there is public agreement over them. In the 21st century we cannot flee any longer. We are going to have to fight for laws and circumstances and environments that allow the free exercise of religion and our franchise in it. ("Israel, Israel, God Is Calling")

No Need to Be Defensive

Hopefully, we can also teach our youth to be confident in their beliefs. Perhaps it was lack of confidence, or lack of testimony that caused those who partook to become ashamed in that critical moment when their actions were mocked. Elder M. Russell Ballard taught:

> In our interactions with others, are we expecting always to have to defend ourselves? If so, I think we need to make a course correction. Constantly anticipating criticism or objections can lead to an unhealthy self-consciousness and a

> defensive posture that doesn't resonate well with others. It is inconsistent with where we are today as a Church and as a great body of followers of Jesus Christ. . . . If we want to be respected today for who we are, then we need to act confidently—secure in the knowledge of who we are and what we stand for, and not as if we have to apologize for our beliefs. ("Sharing the Gospel with Confidence," 46–47)

M. Russell Ballard gave two pieces of advice for those who seek to defend the faith. First, he suggested that "we don't let irrelevant issues drown out the most important subjects." As an example, Elder Ballard mentioned a cable network show about polygamists that depicted a sacred temple ceremony. As an example of how we ought to respond, he cited what the Church officially posted in the lds.org newsroom. "As I quote from it," Elder Ballard said, "listen to the tone. There is nothing defensive about it, yet it was responding to an inappropriate portrayal of one of our most sacred religious ceremonies":

> "Like other large faith groups, The Church of Jesus Christ of Latter-day Saints sometimes

> finds itself on the receiving end of attention from Hollywood or Broadway, television series or books, and the news media. Sometimes depictions of the Church and its people are quite accurate. Sometimes the images are false or play to stereotypes. Occasionally, they are in appallingly bad taste. As Catholics, Jews, and Muslims have known for centuries, such attention is inevitable once an institution or faith group reaches a size or prominence sufficient to attract notice." ("Sharing the Gospel with Confidence," 48)

Often we are questioned about something someone said 150 years ago, or some obscure doctrinal point as if it were the main topic of our lessons in every Sunday School class. Those are irrelevant issues when compared to the first principles of the gospel—faith in the Lord Jesus Christ, repentance, baptism, and the gift of the Holy Ghost.

Elder Ballard's second suggestion was that no matter what the question or concern or criticism may be, we frame our response around our desire to follow Jesus. "Emphasize that Latter-day Saints follow Jesus Christ and what Jesus Christ teaches. We try to follow Him in all that we do." He then gave five short examples of how we might answer questions in this manner, including this one:

> We follow Jesus Christ by adhering to God's law of marriage, which is marriage between a man and a woman. This commandment has been in place from the very beginning. God said, "Therefore shall a man leave his father and his mother, and shall cleave unto his wife: and they shall be one flesh" (Genesis 2:24). God instructed Adam and Eve that they were to "be fruitful, and multiply, and replenish the earth, and subdue it" (Genesis 1:28). ("Sharing the Gospel with Confidence," 51)

By always responding with the Savior in mind, we are helping others focus on the tree of life rather than on the details of the great and spacious building's interior, or on whether the fasteners used to anchor the rod of iron to the ground used straight slot or Phillips heads, or on the degree of incline of one of the many strange roads and forbidden paths out the window that take us nowhere. Just as the sojourners in Lehi's dream were subject to distractions and side roads, we must be sure not to get sidetracked and we should always answer within the context of our testimony of Christ and with Christian love for those asking the questions. The main thing is to keep the main thing the main thing (see Covey, *First Things First,* 75). And the main thing is Jesus Christ and his gospel, and the joy of partaking of the love of God at the tree of life. We desire to follow Jesus.

SEEK "TREE-OF-LIFE MOMENTS"

Before this little book ends, let's move our focus away from the great and spacious and back to the tree "by which we stand."

A friend of mine had an interesting thought while pondering a comment made by Nephi, who mentioned that his family was led by the Liahona to "the more fertile parts of the wilderness" (1 Nephi 16:16). He explained that, like the Liahona, the gospel—and the Church that teaches it—has led him to so many wonderful things, wonderful people, and wonderful experiences.

As I pondered that thought, I realized that my most

cherished experiences were also a direct result of the gospel and the Church. So many and so varied were the experiences that I thought of how abundantly fruitful the tree of life must be to provide spiritual nourishment for all who are willing to come and partake.

Where have your tree-of-life moments come from? Perhaps you find them in a quiet moment in the celestial room, or in a home teaching or visiting teaching moment where the Spirit is present. Perhaps you feel the joy of an act of service pulled off anonymously and beautifully or a musical number that leaves you inspired and introspective.

Much of this book has focused on the great and spacious building, because that's the world where we currently find ourselves. But our spirits will always yearn for more tree-of-life moments, and hopefully the momentary pleasures of the floating and transitory great and spacious building will never have the power to entice us away from the tree of life which is rooted, grounded, and established.

During the time of this writing, I enjoyed Thanksgiving with my extended family. After a scenic drive beneath bright blue skies bordered by wintry mountains, we excitedly entered my sister's country home. My children scattered to the backyard to find cousins, toys, and things to do; I was overcome with the aroma of turkey, stuffing, mashed potatoes, the works. Had an angel walked up and said, "Welcome to Heaven," I would have believed I was there.

After a prayer of gratitude we dished ourselves up, found our places, and began our feast. We ate, we talked, we laughed and enjoyed the company. I continued to marvel at the smells and tastes, and I pondered the kindness of the Lord in giving us such variety! Why did he give us so many different kinds of fruits, so many different kinds of vegetables, so many aromas and flavors? I recalled his generous words:

> Yea, all things which come of the earth, in the season thereof, are made for the benefit and the use of man, both to please the eye and to gladden the heart; Yea, for food and for raiment, for taste and for smell, to strengthen the body and to enliven the soul. And it pleaseth God that he hath given all these things unto man; for unto this end were they made to be used. (D&C 59:18–20)

What a gracious God who created these things to "gladden our hearts" and "enliven our souls." Looking around at my wife and children, my mother, and my brothers and sisters enjoying the meal and the company, I felt such gratitude and joy. We laughed, we reminisced, we remembered our deceased father and grandpa with affection. That moment is frozen in my mind. It was as if my family had been right there with Lehi's family—partaking of the fruit of the tree of life.

Nothing in the great and spacious building could have touched me in that tree-of-life moment. The pride, the wealth, the glitz, the glamour, the bling, the contentious words, the mocking and scoffing—who cares? I would have "heeded them not" without a second thought. It would have been an easy decision and an easy distinction—the lasting joy of the tree of life trumping the temporary pleasure of the great and spacious.

But tree-of-life moments don't last forever. Eventually, the holiday celebration comes to an end, the inspiring conference session closes, the cherished quiet moments in the celestial room give way to the parking lot, and it's back to the lone and dreary world.

Elder Albert E. Bowen observed both the temporary nature of tree-of-life moments and the solution to holding on to their sweetness when he counseled: "When [men] are under the influence of an exalted occasion, they make high resolves. They firmly determine to avoid past mistakes and to do better. But gone out from under the spell of that influence and absorbed in the complicated pursuits of life, they find difficulty in holding fast to their noble purposes. . . . So it is essential that they *come again, and frequently,* under the influence which kindles anew the warmth of spirit in which good resolutions are begotten. . . . Happily, if they refresh themselves frequently enough under ennobling influences, the spirit of repentance will be at work with them, and they will make conquest of some temptations—rise above them—and advance thus far toward their final goal" (Bowen, in Conference Report, October 1949, 139; emphasis added).

That is the answer: Come again and frequently to the tree of life. If there is a chance to feel the Spirit, come again! A chance to hear the pleasing word of God, come again! A chance to fellowship with brothers and sisters, come again! No wonder the counsel is to pray morning, noon, and night, to search the scriptures daily, to take the sacrament weekly, to fast monthly, to visit the temple as frequently as circumstances permit. Each is an opportunity to refresh ourselves at the tree of life, until, as Alma promised, there will be a tree of life springing up in us unto everlasting life (see Alma 33:23).

APPENDIX

Quick Commentary

1 Nephi 8:4–6, 9

- We must go through the wilderness to get to the promised land.
- An angel leads Lehi through darkness, perhaps symbolic of the Fall.
- Prayer delivers us from darkness.

1 Nephi 8:10–12

- The fruit of the tree of life is better than anything else life can offer. There are other enjoyments in the world, but they are temporary. Nothing comes close to the lasting joy the Savior offers.

1 Nephi 8:13–14

- Lehi encountered the tree before noticing anything

else. Not everyone encounters the elements of the dream in the same order, however.

- Sariah, Sam, and Nephi didn't know where to go. Many are "kept from the truth only because they know not where to find it" (D&C 123:12–13).

1 Nephi 8:15–16

- Lehi and the Savior both used the phrase "Come unto me."

1 Nephi 8:18–19

- Laman and Lemuel "would not come" when invited. It was a personal choice on their part. Agency is painful.
- Our first impulse after experiencing something wonderful is to share, which is perhaps the highest motive for missionary work (see Alma 36:24).

1 Nephi 8:19–21

- Lehi makes it clear that he has found where he wants to stay by mentioning the tree "by which I stood" three times.
- Lehi's dream adds an interesting element to the biblical metaphor of the "strait and narrow path," with the introduction of the rod of iron.
- The iron rod is a *guide* rail which leads to the tree, and a *guard* rail which protects us from falling into the river or the depths of hell.

- The path is strait (restricted and narrow) and also straight (undeviating).
- Mists of darkness were a nightmare symbol to ancient Arab poets.
- Lehi describes not just a mist *in* the darkness, but a mist *of* darkness.
- A thick darkness creates a sort of "blindness," not only making it difficult to see, but isolating travelers from others on the path. The effect is loneliness, and the decision to continue or give up becomes an individual one.
- Before the mist of darkness arose, the rod of iron was an unused benefit—with the mist, it becomes the only way to make progress.
- The words *commencing*, *clinging*, and *continuing* may indicate different levels of utilizing the rod of iron.

1 Nephi 8:25–26

- The building is "in the air." Any structure which is "in the air" has no foundation and will eventually fall. In addition, Satan is called "the prince of the power of the air" (Ephesians 2:2), because his influence is "in the very air around us."
- Since the building is up high "in the air," it is the only thing the mists of darkness allow us to see—Satan wants to hide everything else, especially the tree and

the rod of iron; he wants us to see only the building and notice the mocking and scoffing.
- Satan often makes his appearance after great spiritual experiences.

1 Nephi 8:27–28

- Occupants of the building were adorned in costly apparel, implying a worship of wealth over the worship of God.
- While the mists of darkness made it difficult to see, there is nothing in the dream which impaired the travelers' ability to hear. The nearer they came to the tree of life, the more mocking they heard from the great and spacious building.

1 Nephi 8:29–30

- Falling down to partake may indicate both exhaustion and worship.
- Christ is the tree, or the Love of God; evidence that God so loved the world that he gave his only begotten Son (John 3:16).
- "Multitudes" partook, implying that multitudes will be saved.

1 Nephi 8:31–35

- The activity of choice for occupants of the building is to point and mock, although the building is "great and spacious," implying there would be other things to do inside.

- What we "heed" is what separates those who remain at the tree and those who are affected by the lures of the building.

Seeing It All at Once

- All of us are in the dream.
- The entire dream is a grand illustration of Agency.
- The Tree of Life vision is sometimes called "the Parable of the Paths." Jesus' parable of the sower, or the four kinds of soil (see Matthew 13:3–9; Mark 4:3–9; Luke 8:5–8), parallels exactly the four groups described in Lehi's Dream.
- The tree of life is an eternal symbol, since we can't find its beginning (it grew from a seed, which came from a tree, which grew from a seed, and on and on). The building is temporary and man-made, while the tree is something eternal which God grew.
- The tree can be "in us" while we live and work in the world.
- The fountain of living water and the fountain of filthy water illustrate "opposition in all things" (2 Nephi 2:11).
- The dream is a battle of feelings. Some feel joy at the

tree, others feel their way towards the great and spacious building.

Overheard from the Great and Spacious

- "There is no God."
- "There is a God, but he doesn't care what we do."
- "God is Love, so he doesn't punish people."
- "We don't believe in organized religion."
- "You think you're better than us."
- "Why are you trying to convert people?"
- "You're an overzealous fanatic."

But We Heeded Them Not: Not So Simple Anymore

- Help others understand truth.
- Respond with Christian courage.
- No need to be defensive.
- Always answer with the Savior in mind.
- Seek tree-of-life moments.

SOURCES CITED

Asay, Carlos E. "Be Men!" *Ensign,* May 1992, 40–42.

Ballard, M. Russell. *Our Search for Happiness.* Salt Lake City: Deseret Book, 1993.

———. "Sharing the Gospel with Confidence." *Ensign,* July 2010, 45–49.

Bednar, David A. *Increase in Learning.* Salt Lake City: Deseret Book, 2011.

Benson, Ezra Taft. *The Teachings of Ezra Taft Benson.* Salt Lake City: Bookcraft, 1988.

———. "The Power of the Word." *Ensign,* May 1986, 79–82.

Bowen, Albert E. In Conference Report, October 1949, 138–43.

Brickey, Wayne. *Inviting Him In.* Salt Lake City: Deseret Book, 2003.

Bytheway, John. "Weed Your Brain, Grow Your Testimony." Audio CD. Salt Lake City: Deseret Book, 2008.

Cannon, George I. "Live to Make Good Memories." Brigham Young University fireside, 4 August 1991; available at http://speeches.byu.edu/?act=viewitem&id=120; accessed 11 December 2012.

Cook, Quentin L. "Can Ye Feel So Now?" *Ensign*, November 2012, 6–9.

Covey, Stephen R. and A. Roger Merrill and Rebecca R. Merrill. *First Things First.* New York: Free Press, 1994.

Dalton, Elaine S. "At All Times, in All Things, and in All Places." *Ensign*, May 2008, 116–18.

Dickens, Charles. A *Christmas Carol.* Cambridge, MA: Candlewick Press, 2006.

Dobson, James. *Life on the Edge: A Young Adult's Guide to a Meaningful Future.* Nashville, TN: W Publishing Group, 1995.

Eaton, Robert. *Digging Deeper.* Salt Lake City: Deseret Book, 2006.

Faust, James E. *Finding Light in a Dark World.* Salt Lake City: Deseret Book, 1995.

Groberg, John H. *Refuge and Reality: The Blessings of the Temple.* Salt Lake City: Deseret Book, 2012.

Hales, Robert D. "Christian Courage: The Price of Discipleship." *Ensign*, November 2008, 72–75.

Hinckley, Gordon B. "Messages of Inspiration from President Hinckley." *Church News*, July 4, 1998.

Holland, Jeffrey R. *Christ and the New Covenant*. Salt Lake City: Deseret Book, 2006.

———. "Israel, Israel, God Is Calling." CES devotional, 16 September 2012; available at http://www.lds.org/broadcasts/article/ces-devotionals/2012/01/israel-israel-god-is-calling?lang=eng; accessed 10 December 2012.

———. "The Ministry of Angels." *Ensign*, November 2008, 29–31.

Hymns of The Church of Jesus Christ of Latter-day Saints. Salt Lake City: The Church of Jesus Christ of Latter-day Saints, 1985.

Johnston, Jerry Earl. "'Designer Faith' Trend Here to Stay." *Deseret News*, November 25, 2012.

Journal of Discourses. 26 vols. London: Latter-day Saints' Book Depot, 1856–86.

Largey, Dennis. *The Book of Mormon Reference Companion*. Salt Lake City: Deseret Book, 2012.

"Living by the Scriptures." *Church News*, August 16, 1997.

Lund, Gerald N. *Jesus Christ: Key to the Plan of Salvation*. Salt Lake City: Deseret Book, 1991.

Maxwell, Neal A. *Neal A. Maxwell Quote Book*. Cory Maxwell, ed. Salt Lake City: Deseret Book, 1997.

———. "Overcome . . . Even As I Also Overcame." *Ensign*, May 1987, 70–72.

———.*The Smallest Part*. Salt Lake City: Deseret Book, 1973.

McConkie, Bruce R. *Doctrinal New Testament Commentary*. Vol. 2. Salt Lake City: Bookcraft, 1971.

McConkie, Joseph Fielding. *Seeking the Spirit*. Salt Lake City: Bookcraft, 1978.

McConkie, Joseph Fielding and Robert L. Millet. *Doctrinal Commentary on the Book of Mormon*. 4 Vols. Salt Lake City: Bookcraft, 1987–1992.

Millet, Robert L. *Lehi's Dream*. Salt Lake City: Deseret Book, 2001.

Nibley, Hugh. *Ancient Documents and the Pearl of Great Price*. Kindle edition. Salt Lake City: Deseret Book, 2010.

———. *Lehi in the Desert/The World of the Jaredites/There Were Jaredites*. Edited by John W. Welch with Darrell L. Matthews and Stephen R. Callister. Salt Lake City and Provo: Deseret Book Co., Foundation for Ancient Research and Mormon Studies, 1988.

Oaks, Dallin H. "Judge Not and Judging." *Brigham Young*

University Speeches 1997–98. Provo: Brigham Young University Press, 1998.

———. "Love and Law." *Ensign*, November 2009, 26–29.

Packer, Boyd K. "Counsel to Youth." *Ensign*, November 2011, 16–19.

———. "Finding Ourselves in Lehi's Dream." *Ensign*, August 2010, 21–25.

———. "Lehi's Dream and You." BYU devotional, 16 January 2007; available at http://speeches.byu.edu/?act=viewitem&id=1673; accessed 10 December 2012.

———. *Mine Errand from the Lord*. Salt Lake City: Deseret Book, 2008.

Roberts, B. H. *A Comprehensive History of The Church of Jesus Christ of Latter-day Saints*. 6 vols. Salt Lake City: The Church of Jesus Christ of Latter-day Saints, 1957.

Satterfield, Bruce. "Lehi's Dream: The Indispensable Foundation of the Book of Mormon." Unpublished manuscript. Used by permission.

Smith, Joseph. *History of The Church of Jesus Christ of Latter-day Saints*. 7 vols. Ed. B. H. Roberts. Salt Lake City: The Church of Jesus Christ of Latter-day Saints, 1932–51.

———. *Teachings of the Prophet Joseph Smith*. Ed. Joseph Fielding Smith. Salt Lake City: Deseret Book, 1976.

Uchtdorf, Dieter F. "The Merciful Obtain Mercy." *Ensign*, May 2012, 70–77.

Welch, John. "Study, Faith, and the Book of Mormon." *BYU Today*, September 1988: 22.

Wilcox, Brad. *Learning (Not Earning) Heaven*. Audio CD. Salt Lake City: Deseret Book, 2012.

Wilcox, S. Michael. *Don't Leap with the Sheep*. Salt Lake City: Deseret Book, 2001.

Yorgason, Blaine M. *Spiritual Progression in the Last Days*. Salt Lake City: Deseret Book, 1994.

Ziglar, Zig. *See You at the Top*. Gretna, LA: Pelican Publishing, 2005.

INDEX

ABOUT THE AUTHOR

JOHN BYTHEWAY served a mission to the Philippines and later graduated from Brigham Young University. A favorite speaker and teacher, John holds a master's degree in Religious Education and is a part-time instructor at BYU. John is the author of many bestselling books, audio talks, and DVDs, including three scripture commentaries: *Of Pigs, Pearls, and Prodigals: A Fresh Look at the Parables of Jesus*; *Isaiah for Airheads*; and *Righteous Warriors: Lessons from the War Chapters in the Book of Mormon*. He and his wife, Kimberly, have six children.